All
About
Christmas

Dorothy Nicolle

Illustrated by
Peter Clayton

*I will honour Christmas
in my heart
and try to keep it all the year.*

(Ebenezer Scrooge,
on seeing his grave,
in *A Christmas Carol*)

Blue Hills Press

© Text - Dorothy Nicolle 2011
© Illustrations - Peter Clayton 2011

ISBN 978-0-9560293-7-9

Published by:
Blue Hills Press, 32 Chapel Street, Wem
Shropshire SY4 5ER
www.bluehillspress.co.uk

Printed by:
Cambrian Printers, Llanbadar Road
Aberystwyth SY23 3TN

Contents

*Our old English anniversary
of smiles.*
(Illustrated London News, 1800s)

Any biblical quotes in this book
have been taken from the
King James Authorised Version of the Bible.

1
The first Christmas

Let us now go even unto Bethlehem.
(Luke, Chapter 2)

Jesus was born in… well, which year was it… was it 1 BC or 1 AD? We know he was born on 25 December… or do we? In fact, as soon as we try to work out the exact date and year of His birth we start to hit snags.

There are some things we do have accurate dates for, however. For example we know that King Herod died in what we now regard as the year 4 BC. Oh! But he was alive when Jesus was born, so how can that be? There's something wrong somewhere. When you start to look into the detail it soon becomes very clear that we just don't have any accurate details at all about when Jesus was born.

So is there any way of working out when the Christmas story took place? Indeed there is. Many people have turned detective and tried to sort out this puzzle and, invariably, they have come up with many conflicting ideas. So, let's try to sort out the muddle. What facts do we have?

We know, as a historical fact, that King Herod died in 4 BC so Jesus must have been born before his death.

We also know from the story in the Bible that Mary and Joseph were in Bethlehem at the time of the birth of Jesus, having been told to go there in order to be counted – a census was taking place. There would appear to be no records of when this census took place but historians have come to the conclusion that it probably happened between the years 11 BC and 7 BC.

And it came to pass in those days, that there went out a decree
from Caesar Augustus, that all the world should be taxed.
(Luke, Chapter 2)

These days we tend to think of a census as an event that takes place every ten years on one specified day when everyone in the country fills in a form giving personal details on that specific date. In the ancient world, however, things were rather different. A census could take years to be completed – for example one census in Gaul under the Roman Empire took four decades before it was completed. Thus, if a census was taken in Judaea sometime between the years 11 BC and 7 BC it could well have overrun by up to three or four years.

This doesn't really help us to ascertain the exact date when Jesus was born except that it agrees roughly with the dates when King Herod ruled the region and is not long before he died.

Is there any other way in which we can find out the date? Another event at the time that is mentioned in the Bible is the sighting of that famous star by the three wise men. The appearance of such a star must have been noticed in many parts of the world. Was it a star, or was it perhaps a comet – what exactly was it that they saw?

> *Now when Jesus was born in Bethlehem of Judaea in the days*
> *of Herod the king, behold, there came wise men from the east to*
> *Jerusalem, saying, Where is he that is born King of the Jews? for*
> *we have seen his star in the east, and are come to worship him.*
> (Matthew, Chapter 2)

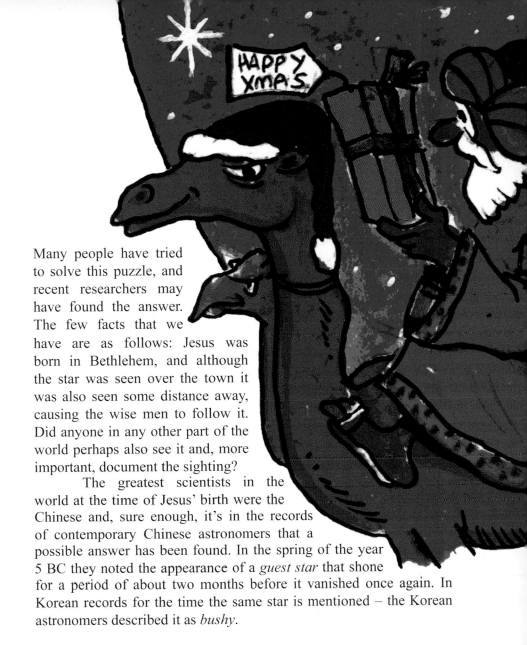

Many people have tried to solve this puzzle, and recent researchers may have found the answer. The few facts that we have are as follows: Jesus was born in Bethlehem, and although the star was seen over the town it was also seen some distance away, causing the wise men to follow it. Did anyone in any other part of the world perhaps also see it and, more important, document the sighting?

The greatest scientists in the world at the time of Jesus' birth were the Chinese and, sure enough, it's in the records of contemporary Chinese astronomers that a possible answer has been found. In the spring of the year 5 BC they noted the appearance of a *guest star* that shone for a period of about two months before it vanished once again. In Korean records for the time the same star is mentioned – the Korean astronomers described it as *bushy*.

> *...and, lo, the star, which they saw in the east, went before them,*
> *till it came and stood over where the young child was.*
> (Matthew, Chapter 2)

And what was this star? – it's now thought that it must have been a supernova, an exploding star in the distant heavens, which would explain why it was only seen for a relatively short period of time.

There's also a suggestion that the Bethlehem star was a really bright light in the heavens caused by the conjunction of three stars or planets in October of 7 BC. But I prefer the 5 BC date because it fits with further research that has also thrown up the information that the Jewish festival of Passover in that same year was held in the month of April. Passover was a time when families tried to get together, so it would have been a convenient time to carry out a census. This, then, could be the reason why it was chosen for the census that was held in Bethlehem. It would also explain why the little town was full of people that spring, so that Joseph was unable to find a place at the inn for his pregnant wife, Mary.

Another clue from the Bible that reminds us that Jesus was indeed born in the springtime is the reference to the shepherds watching their sheep by night. In the middle of winter the sheep would have been brought down from the hills and then, as soon as spring approached, they would have been taken out to feed on the new grass. The shepherds would need to watch them carefully at this time of year because this is the lambing season, a very busy time for shepherds everywhere.

And she brought forth her first-born son, and wrapped
him in swaddling clothes, and laid him in a manger;
because there was no room for them in the inn.
(Luke, Chapter 2)

But I keep talking about springtime. Surely Jesus was born in December, in other words, in the middle of winter? No. From all the evidence, we really have to accept that He was probably born in the **spring** of the year 5 BC.

And so we are then left with the puzzle of why we celebrate His birth in December.

The December date came about for several different reasons. In the early years of Christianity the story of Jesus' birth was largely ignored. His teachings during His life and, most important of all, the manner of His death, were considered to be far more significant facets of the new religion than any stories about His birth, and it was on these that early Christianity focused.

It was in the 4th century that the decision was made to celebrate Christ's birth in December. Christians at this time considered that the new year began around the time of the Spring Equinox. But then the Church realised that before He was born Jesus must first have been conceived, and Mary must then have had a pregnancy of nine months. It was therefore decided that His conception would have occurred in springtime, something that we still celebrate each year on Lady Day, 25 March. Add on nine months … and you reach Christmas Day.

The birth of Jesus on Christmas Day, so close to the Winter Solstice, was fortuitous for another reason. The days just after the Winter Solstice were traditionally days of hope for our pagan ancestors – the worst of the winter weather might still be ahead, but from then on the days would start to lengthen, and there was the promise that springtime was approaching.

Consequently, it had long been the tradition amongst different pagan cultures to celebrate the passing of the Winter Solstice. For example, the Romans celebrated with a festival that they called *Saturnalia*, after the god Saturn – it was a time of riotous celebration with feasting and merrymaking, and it lasted for several days from 17 to 23 December.

Another Roman god, one that originated in Persia, was the god Mithras. His *Festival of the Birthday of the Unconquered Sun* was already celebrated on 25 December. There are a number of other analogies with Jesus here – Mithras had supposedly been born with shepherds attending his birth, he had a Last Supper, and his adherents believed that he would one day rise from the dead and return to his people. Of course this last claim is a common one in many religions and legends from around the world – think of our own claims about King Arthur!

By the 4th century Christian missionaries were carrying the ideas of the new religion all around the Roman Empire. It was soon realised by these missionaries that it would be easier for those pagans they were converting to absorb the new religion if it could be closely linked with elements of the old. The time of the rebirth of the Sun, which was already being celebrated, could thus easily be linked with the time of the birth of the Son of God.

And so, the celebration of Christ's Mass came to be connected with the earlier and long-established Winter Solstice festivals. This also, of course, goes a long way to explaining why there are so many pagan elements about Christmas as we celebrate it today.

There was a tabby cat in the stable at Bethlehem. At one time, when the infant Jesus began to cry, the cat soothed him back to sleep with the sound of its purring. Mary then stroked the cat, leaving a mark like an initial M on the cat's forehead. Ever since then this mark has been found on every tabby cat.

The word *Christmas*, derived from *Christ's Mass*, was first coined in the 11th century by the Norman invaders of England.Centuries later Puritans, who denounced the celebration of Christmas, referred to it instead as Saturn's Mass. In this way they emphasised two elements that they totally disapproved of – the festivities associated with Christmas were deemed by them to be both pagan (the god Saturn) and Catholic (Mass).

Merry Xmas! How often have you winced when you've seen that word *Xmas* and thought of it as a dumbed-down word for Christmas? Actually, it was a shorthand form of the word for Christmas used by monks in medieval times. Also, in Greek "X" is the first letter of Christ's name and so became a holy symbol in itself.

It was in an Armenian gospel dating from the 6th century that the three kings were first identified by name. Melkon (or Melchior) was the King of the Persians, Gaspar (or Caspar) was the King of the Hindus and Balthazar was the King of the Arabs. This early account also describes how they arrived from Persia accompanied by 12,000 soldiers. No wonder King Herod was a bit alarmed!

Other, later texts describe Melchior as King of the Persians, Caspar as King of Tarsus (in present-day Turkey) and Balthazar as King of the Ethiopians. Then there is a 15th century chronicle that says it was Caspar who came from Ethiopia. It's all a bit of a muddle.

The word *Magi* comes from the Greek *magoi* which, itself, comes from a Persian word and originally referred to priests of the ancient Zoroastrian religion in that country. Such priests were men who would have used astrology in their arts. This is also where our modern word *magic* comes from.

2

Christmas decorations

The holly and the ivy,
Now both are full well grown,
Of all the trees that are in the wood,
The holly bears the crown.

It is when we look at the way we decorate our houses at Christmas time, that we are immediately struck by the numerous pagan survivals in everything that we do. Holly, ivy, mistletoe – the symbolism behind each of them is purely pagan; in fact any *Christian* symbolism has been invented relatively recently to make such things more acceptable to those who abhor the idea of pagan elements in our ritual.

Holly and ivy

Holly and ivy have been used since Celtic times to decorate our houses at the time of the Winter Solstice. It's winter; the trees have all lost their leaves; everything looks dead. And yet holly looks its best, with its shiny green leaves and bright red berries. No wonder our ancestors thought the plant was magical.

The Romans thought the same, and at this time of year (during their festival of Saturnalia) they would exchange gifts decorated with sprigs of holly since they believed that the plant would repel evil spirits.

There are many legends associated with holly. It was said that a cane made from the wood of the holly would protect maidens from wild dogs and vicious beasts. Another legend said that holly had the power to ward off witches. Bringing it into the house at Midwinter also calmed any goblins that lived with you and prevented them from causing mischief, perhaps because it was in the holly that the fairies and elves were believed to live.

With the advent of Christianity, holly took on new associations. The prickly leaves of the holly reminded people of the crown of thorns worn by Jesus as He walked to Calvary and the red berries were therefore said to represent His blood. In fact a legend grew up saying that holly berries were originally yellow but were stained red by the blood of Jesus when they were used for His crown of thorns.

Ivy, too, had its own legends and traditions. Bacchus, the god of drink, always wore a crown made from ivy because it was said to ward off drunkenness. It's also said that if you place an ivy leaf in a bowl of water on New Year's Eve and leave it and it remains fresh and green until Twelfth Night, you are assured of a good and healthy year ahead. If any black spots appear, however, it warns that there will be illness and possibly a death in the family.

Holly and ivy also represent the two sexes – holly is said to be male and ivy female. (I have, however, come across a reference where these attributes are reversed!) Whichever may be true, it became the tradition to use the plants entwined together when decorating your house to represent unity between men and women.

Unity is all very well, but you should take care when and how you bring your decorations into the house. It's considered bad luck to bring holly or ivy into the house before 24 December – it will cause quarrels if brought in too soon. Moreover, if you want to be in control of your household in the coming year, there are certain rules you should follow – in fact there are three different traditions in play here.

One states that since holly represents men and ivy represents women, whichever of these two is brought first into the house will dictate who will rule the household. If, however, you look at the different kinds of holly available in the market you will see that some plants are very prickly and some much less so, and so a second tradition states that the prickly holly represents men (naturally!) and the non-prickly represents women, and it is whichever of these you choose to decorate your house with which will decide who rules the household.

The third tradition is, perhaps, the simplest one to follow – the person to rule the household in the coming year will be the person who first carries the holly indoors.

Priests in ancient Greece gave ivy wreaths to newlyweds as a sign of fidelity.

In the 18th century ivy was considered a token of melancholy; perhaps this came about because of its association with gravestones.

Farmers were always careful not to fell a holly tree completely - to remove its roots was to risk having its place being taken by a witch.

Some facts about holly and ivy

Holly (*Ilex aquifolium*) is the most common of Britain's native evergreens. The word *holly* comes from an Old English word *hollin*.

Holly berries are poisonous but were sometimes used as an emetic.

Although it may look an unlikely foodstuff with its sharp, prickly leaves, holly has long been used as fodder for animals in winter when other food is scarce. If you look at a holly tree you will notice that the leaves towards the top are not so sharp – these are more digestible, and farmers would often cut them down for their livestock. The spiky leaves lower down are, in fact, a defensive measure on the part of the tree to prevent animals from eating the leaves they can reach.

Holly wood is good for firewood, even when it is green.

Ivy (its Latin name is *Hedera helix*) can live in colonies that are thousands of years old.

Mistletoe

It has been writ that any man
May kiss whatever girl he can,
And nobody shall tell him 'No'
Beneath the holy mistletoe.

So, ladies, be careful where you stand at Christmas time! Mind you, if an unmarried girl stands under the mistletoe and no-one kisses her, she will remain unmarried for the coming year.

So how did this tradition come about, and why should mistletoe be so special?

The mistletoe plant (*Viscum album*) is a parasite most commonly found growing on apple trees. It gets its name from the Old English *mistel* and *tang* meaning *dung* and *twig* (literally *dung on a twig*, which isn't in the least romantic) since people had noticed that this plant grew on trees where birds had left their droppings. Although poisonous to us, birds eat the berries and then deposit the seeds on the trees.

Mistletoe, since it's an evergreen and has luscious berries in the midst of winter, came to be seen by the Druids as having magical powers; it was a giver of life. A tree with mistletoe growing on it was therefore considered to have been touched by the gods. The Druids also worshipped oak trees, so that when a mistletoe plant was found growing on an oak tree it was thought to be especially powerful. We know they would cut mistletoe down from the tree using a golden sickle, taking care to ensure that when it fell it landed on a white cloth and wasn't contaminated by touching the earth. But, otherwise, we don't know just how the Druids used mistletoe in their rituals.

There is a legend in Norse mythology that perhaps explains why we associate mistletoe with love and romance. The goddess Freya (from whom we get our word *Friday*) gave birth to a boy, whom she named Balder. Freya was obsessed with anxiety for the safety of her son, and so she made all creatures and plants on Earth promise to do him no harm. Because Balder

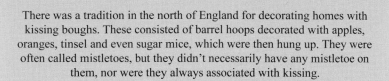

There was a tradition in the north of England for decorating homes with kissing boughs. These consisted of barrel hoops decorated with apples, oranges, tinsel and even sugar mice, which were then hung up. They were often called mistletoes, but they didn't necessarily have any mistletoe on them, nor were they always associated with kissing.

Another name for mistletoe was *the plant of the moon*, its white berries being an obvious explanation for this name. In Brittany, on the other hand, the mistletoe is called *Herbe de la Croix* because it was thought that Christ's Cross was made from mistletoe wood. The plant was so ashamed of such a terrible association with Jesus that it shrank to its present size. This is why mistletoe should never be used to decorate a church. However, at York Minster there used to be a special annual Mistletoe Service in the winter at which wrongdoers in the city would be pardoned. Until recently a sprig of mistletoe was placed on the altar each Christmas – a tradition unique to the Minster.

Mistletoe was considered to have magical properties. Supposedly, it was capable of breaking the trances of epileptics. It was also said to protect your home from witchcraft – it kept the witches away from your meat and fleas away from your bed. It also prevented fairies from snatching away your babies.

In some parts of the country the mistletoe would be burnt on Twelfth Night because otherwise those boys and girls who had kissed under it would never get married. Farmers, on the other hand, would sometimes keep the mistletoe used at Christmas and give it to the first cow that calved in the spring. This would then bring good luck to the entire herd.

In the Middle Ages women who wanted to conceive would tie mistletoe around their waist or wrists in order to increase their fertility.

couldn't be harmed, the other gods would often use him as a target when they were practising aiming their weapons.

But one god, Loki, was jealous of Balder, and he realised that Freya had forgotten to get the mistletoe plant to promise never to harm her son. So he made a lance tipped with mistletoe and gave it to Balder's blind brother, Hadr, to throw. Guided by Loki, Hadr's lance struck Balder and killed him.

Winter descended on the land. But then the other gods brought Balder back to life, and Freya was so grateful that she declared that from then onwards mistletoe should always bring love rather than death to the world, and people passing under the plant should embrace. So the custom grew that warring parties, when they met to discuss an armistice, should lay down their arms under a mistletoe plant.

Which perhaps explains why we kiss under the mistletoe. But, inevitably, there are a number of rules which govern how we use mistletoe. As with holly and ivy it's unlucky, for example, to bring it into the house before Christmas Eve. The first kiss under the mistletoe should be between people who have hair of different colour. And that first kiss should not be between a man and his wife.

Pick a berry off the mistletoe
For ev'ry kiss that's given.
When the berries have all gone,
There's an end to kissing.

And there is one other rule which should always be observed – each time a kiss is taken under the mistletoe, a berry should be removed from the plant. Once the berries have all gone the kissing has to stop.

The average person
burns off
26 calories in a
one-minute kiss!

18

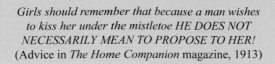

Some facts about mistletoe

Mistletoe is a parasite and grows on many types of deciduous trees including apple, rowan and hawthorn. It was considered most sacred when found growing on an oak tree. It is said that, in all of Britain, there are only eleven oak trees with mistletoe growing on them and seven of them are to be found in Herefordshire.

Mistletoe is a pure plant with no hybrids. The berries, which are eaten by birds like the mistle thrush or blackbird, pass through their digestive systems, and the sticky seeds are then deposited on trees in their droppings. The seed then develops and eventually its roots tap into the sap system of the tree.

Mistletoe has separate male and female plants.

Mistletoe berries do not usually ripen until springtime, although there are always some berries that have ripened by Christmas.

Mistletoe takes a long time to grow – it often takes up to five years before a plant has any berries on it.

There are at least 2,000 species of mistletoe within three families. In the United States one species, *Phoradendron flavescens*, is the state flower of Oklahoma.

Today mistletoe is classed as one of Britain's hundred most endangered plants. Therefore, if you must pick some in the wild, always ensure that you leave some of the plant growing in the tree so that it will regenerate.

Tenbury Wells in Worcestershire is the world's mistletoe capital. Each year, just before Christmas, mistletoe markets are held near the town and from here it is sent all over the world.

There's an old wives' tale that if you drink mistletoe berries that have been crushed in (male) urine, you will get rid of jaundice! But I wouldn't advise you to try this – the berries are actually poisonous. Today, however, a new medical use has been found for mistletoe – lectin from the berries is now used for the treatment of cancer. It has also recently been discovered that it can kill bacteria that have developed a resistance to antibiotics.

In Irish and Scots Gaelic, the word for mistletoe translates as *all-heal*.

There is now a National Mistletoe Day. It was endorsed by Parliament in 2005 and takes place on 1 December each year.

Other plants associated with Christmas

There are a number of other plants that are traditionally associated with Christmas. Although now used as a seasoning for food **rosemary**, for example, used to be spread on the floor of houses to give fragrance as people walked over it (an early form of *pot pourri*). And how did the plant get its scent in the first place? It's said that on the flight to Egypt, Mary washed some of Jesus' clothes and laid them on a plant to dry causing it to produce the sweet scent; this also explains why the small flowers of the rosemary plant are the same colour, blue, as Mary's robe.

Furthermore, no matter how long it lives, rosemary will never grow taller than Jesus, and if it should live for more than 33 years (the equivalent of His lifespan) it will then grow outwards rather than upwards.

Laurel (or **bay**) was sacred to the sun god, Apollo, and was used long ago to decorate houses for Midwinter festivals as a reminder that the long winter would soon become spring.

A tropical plant that is now closely associated with Christmas is the **poinsettia**. Legend has it that some poor children wanted to decorate a crib in their church one Christmas but couldn't afford to buy anything. Instead they picked some green plants growing by the roadside and used these as decoration around the crib. On Christmas morning, when they returned to the church, they discovered that the green leaves had miraculously turned into a glorious deep red colour.

Another plant is so closely linked with Christmas that it even has the word *Christmas* as part of its name. Legend has it that the **Christmas rose** bloomed outside the stable in Bethlehem when Jesus was born, but in fact it isn't native to that area at all.

A similar story to that of the poinsettia tells of how a young girl came to visit the baby but, she too, couldn't afford a gift, and so she started to weep. Her tears fell on a plant poking through the snow, whereupon it turned into flowers which she then presented to Mary and Jesus - hence the Christmas rose.

Some facts about poinsettias

The flower of the plant is actually the yellow centre, the red *petals* are really the leaves of the plant.

The Aztecs called the plant *cuetlaxochitl* and for them it symbolised blood sacrifices.

The poinsettia is named for Joel Robert Poinsett who was the United States ambassador serving in Mexico in the 1820s.

Poinsettias were known as the *Flower of Christmas Eve* and were thought to symbolise the Star of Bethlehem.

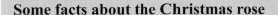

Some facts about the Christmas rose

The Christmas rose is one of Britain's oldest cultivated plants and is thought to have been introduced to the country by the Romans.

This plant is very poisonous. Its botanical name is *Helleborus niger*. The first part of its name comes from Greek words meaning to kill (*hellin*) and food (*bora*). The Romans are thought to have rubbed hellebore on their arrows.

Until comparatively recent times it was used as a medicine to cure worms in children – it was certainly effective in killing the worms but often, if too much was used, it killed the children too.

It is said that you should plant Christmas roses near to your house to keep witches and evil spirits away; it also prevents thunderbolts from striking the house.

Until the 17th century the Christmas rose was thought to be a cure for insanity, and it was also used to treat cattle that had been put under a spell.

Some facts about rosemary

Rosemary is said to have been first introduced into England in the 14th century by Philippa of Hainault, the wife of King Edward III. Perhaps this connection with a queen explains why it grows best in a kitchen garden where a woman reigns supreme!

Rosemary is used in the treatment of dandruff.

In Shakespeare's *Hamlet* rosemary symbolises remembrance. It's also said to aid memory, so that, in ancient Greece students would wear it in their hair when taking examinations.

The wreath that you hang on your door at Christmas symbolises the strength of life overcoming the forces of winter. Having no beginning or end, it also represents eternity. Hanging a wreath on your door is an ancient tradition and probably comes from the Romans who used wreaths as a sign of victory and celebration.

There is another plant in England that has a special association with Christmas – the **Glastonbury Thorn**. This was a hawthorn that grew in the grounds of Glastonbury Abbey. Once, so the story goes, Joseph of Arimathea was visiting Somerset (he was a merchant touring local tin mines) and, on his arrival, he sat down to rest. As he did so he pushed his wooden staff into the ground nearby. Once he had rested, he got up and continued on his way, leaving the staff behind.

It so happened that this staff had been made from wood from the very same tree that was used to make the crown of thorns that Jesus wore when He went to Calvary. Miraculously the staff took root and from it grew a hawthorn tree and, in memory of its association with Jesus, it always flowered at Christmas time.

Over the years a tradition grew up of giving a hawthorn blossom to the monarch each Christmas, but this custom ended during the reign of Charles I. It was revived in 1922 when a flowering sprig from the tree was presented to Queen Mary.

Sadly, the tree died in 1991 and was subsequently cut down. Many people tried to grow new hawthorn plants from the seeds of this one, and they were often successful, but none of these plants ever repeated the miracle of producing blossoms at Christmas time. Fortunately, however, some new trees had been grafted from the original,

The original Glastonbury Thorn from Joseph of Arimathea's staff grew on Wearyall Hill, just to the south of Glastonbury. It was cut down by Puritans in the 1600s because they deemed it an object of superstition. This means that the Glastonbury thorn at Glastonbury Abbey must have grown from a cutting from the original plant. In 1800 a plaque was put on the site on Wearyall Hill to show where the first plant used to grow.

Joseph of Arimathea was a rich Jew who, at the time of Jesus' Crucifixion, was a secret disciple of Jesus. It was he who went to Pontius Pilate after the Crucifixion and asked for the body of Jesus, so that it could be placed in the new tomb he had already had cut in the rock for his own body when he should die himself.
Legend has it that it was Joseph of Arimathea who founded the first Christian church in England at Glastonbury, which would have been long before Christianity historically came to Britain.
Another legend says that it was Joseph who kept the cup that Jesus drank from at the Last Supper – known to history as the Holy Grail – and it was he who brought it to England.
Yet another legend tells us that it was Joseph who brought a little brown bird with a red breast with him when he came here – a bird that has since become closely associated in our minds with Christmas.

and occasionally some of these do indeed produce flowers in time for Christmas. And when they do, a sprig with blossom on it is given to the Queen and takes pride of place decorating her table when she sits down for her Christmas dinner.

And when do you take your Christmas decorations down?

Down with the rosemary, and so
Down with the bays and mistletoe;
Down with the holly, ivy and all
Wherewith ye dress'd the Christmas hall;
That so the superstitious find
Not one least branch there left behind;
For look, how many leaves there be
Neglected there, maids, trust to me,
So many goblins you shall see.
(Robert Herrick, in the 17th century)

So when should you take your decorations down? Originally decorations were kept up until Candlemas (2 February) but these days most of us agree that decorations should come down by Twelfth Night. I'm sure you won't be surprised to learn, however, that there are many other traditions associated with the removal of your decorations.

In some parts of Ireland the decorations used to be left up until Shrove Tuesday. They would then be taken down and burnt in the fire over which the pancakes were cooked.

In other places the decorations would be kept up all year to protect the house from lightning – this custom still survives in one sense, as I have come across many people who deliberately leave just one sprig of holly behind the back of a picture until the following year. In Herefordshire it was mistletoe that was kept up all year, only being removed when you replaced it the following year and burnt the old piece in your fire.

3
Christmas trees

*In the middle of the room stood an immense tub with
a yew tree placed in it, from the branches of which
hung bunches of sweet-meats, almonds,
and raisins, in papers,
fruit and toys, most tastefully arranged,
and the whole illuminated by small wax candles.*
(John Watkins, biographer of Queen Charlotte,
describing her Christmas tree)

Doesn't everyone know that Prince Albert, the consort of Queen
Victoria, introduced the Christmas tree to England in the 1840s? Well,
everyone is wrong then – it was actually Queen Charlotte (the wife of
King George III) who first had a Christmas tree in England, in the year
1761. Princess Victoria, before her marriage to Albert, had therefore
already grown up with the tradition of Christmas trees. In her journal of
1833, Victoria (then aged 14) refers to *two large round tables on which
were placed trees hung with lights and sugar ornaments*.

So, it would be more accurate to say that it was Prince Albert
who *popularised* the Christmas tree in this country when, with the
Queen and their children, he posed in front of a tree for a photograph
in 1848. The photograph was published all over the country so that,
in the years that followed, everyone wanted a Christmas tree, to be
like the Queen. In fact, the idea of having a Christmas tree in your
front parlour took the country by storm and, as early as 1850, Charles
Dickens described a Christmas tree as *that pretty German toy* because,
like many of our Christmas traditions, the decoration of Christmas trees
is not only an ancient pagan practice but has also come from Germany.

Outside of court circles, the Christmas tree was already known
in England before Victoria's reign. As early as 1789, in her diary, a
Mrs Papendiek recorded that her husband *proposed an illuminated tree
according to the German tradition* in their house for the festivities. We

also know that in Manchester, German merchants in the 1830s had trees for decorative purposes at Christmas.

The first written evidence of a Christmas tree anywhere is to be found in a diary of a man who visited Strasbourg (then part of Germany) in 1605. He wrote *At Christmas they set up fir-trees in the parlours of Strasbourg and hang thereon roses cut out of many-coloured papers, apples, wafers, gold-foil, sweets and so on.*

By 1800 Christmas trees had become popular in Finland and they were known in Denmark and Norway by 1830 and then in France by 1840. But Christmas trees were known in the United States even before this time – Hessian mercenaries had taken the tradition to America with them when they went to fight in the War of Independence.

It's thought that the ancient Celts in Germany first decorated these trees in order to encourage the tree spirits, that had apparently abandoned the other trees when they lost their leaves. This belief is also probably behind our own pagan tradition of tree-dressing. Tree-dressing ceremonies used to take place in England on Oak Apple Day. It so happens that Oak Apple Day (29 May) was also the day on which Charles II arrived in London to claim his throne in 1660. And so, to commemorate his escape after the Battle of Worcester in 1651 by hiding in an oak tree, many people revived the old tradition and decorated trees to celebrate the King's return. One tree (though not an oak tree but a black poplar) is still dressed and decorated with flags each year on this date, in Aston-on-Clun in Shropshire.

The Christian association with these trees is said to date back to the time of St Boniface in the 8th century. The legend is that one day he came across some men who were about to cut down such a tree to use as a stake for a human sacrifice. With a mighty blow St Boniface felled the tree, but as it split apart a new young fir tree sprang from its heart. St Boniface told the pagans that the tree was holy and symbolised the promise of eternal life that came with Christianity. History doesn't tell us, however, what happened to the man who was to be sacrificed!

The most famous of all our Christmas trees is surely the one that adorns Trafalgar Square in London each year. Every Christmas, since 1947, the people of Norway have presented a tree to the people of the United Kingdom in gratitude for Britain's help during the Second World War.

Some facts about Christmas trees

The classic Christmas tree is the Norway spruce which was introduced to Britain around 1500.

It takes a Christmas tree between seven and ten years to grow to maturity, and some three seedlings are usually planted for each tree that is eventually harvested.

The Norway spruce can grow to a height of over 60 ft.

One acre of Christmas trees provides enough oxygen for 18 people for one day.

In 1851 the first commercial sale of trees (in the United States) took place in New York City. Mark Carr from the Catskill Mountains, north of New York, realised that there was a ready market in the city for mountain-cut trees. He took two sleds laden with trees and was quickly sold out. He returned every year with his trees and, 30 years later, there were over 600 dealers selling trees in the city.

By the 1890s Christmas tree markets were being held in London's Covent Garden. One retailer's records show that he could supply trees up to 40 ft (12.2m) in height and his sales topped 30,000 trees every year.

The first tree farm was planted in the early 1900s near Trenton in New Jersey by WV McGalliard. He planted some 25,000 Norway spruce. A few years later, customers were allowed to select and cut their own trees, a tradition which continues today on both sides of the Atlantic. By the end of the century, some 36 million trees were harvested each year in North America alone. In Britain serious commercial production of Christmas trees began only in the 1960s.

In Great Britain, since 1982, it has been the British Christmas Tree Growers Association that provides Downing Street with a tree each year. Similarly, the American Forestry Association donates a tree each year to the White House. They gave their first tree in 1923 and it was lit by President and Mrs Coolidge.

The first artificial Christmas trees were made from feathers, usually turkey or goose feathers, sometimes even ostrich and swan feathers. The feathers were dyed, the quills were stripped from them and they were then individually wired onto wooden branches. These trees were sometimes known as *Nuremberg Christmas trees* because it was in Nuremberg, in Germany, that they originated.

In the 1930s the Addis Brush Company in the United States began to produce artificial trees. These were made using the same bristles they used to make toilet brushes. The bristles were dyed green and the trees were known as *bottlebrush trees*. They proved to be very successful because they were stronger than the earlier feather trees and could support ornaments better.

The Parker family of Wiltshire claims to own the world's oldest artificial Christmas tree. It was bought in 1886 and is still used every year.

In the oil industry a *Christmas tree* is the name given to the set of valves over an oil well by means of which the flow of oil is controlled.

If you cut a pine cone lengthwise you will find inside it what appears to be the imprint of a tiny hand, the hand, so it's said, of the infant Jesus. The story is that, as they fled from Herod's soldiers to Egypt, the Holy Family at one time hid within the trunk of a hollowed pine tree. When the soldiers had gone by and it was safe for the family to leave, Jesus blessed the tree and the imprint of His hand remains to this day.

It's said that the tree of life in the Garden of Eden was a fir tree. When Eve plucked its fruit, however, the foliage and flowers shrank to become the needles that we know today. Only on the anniversary of Jesus' birth can the fir tree bloom once more, as it does when we decorate such trees. Perhaps this explains why, in medieval mystery plays a sacred, or paradise, tree was used as a symbol of the Garden of Eden. These were usually fir trees and they were often hung with apples and surrounded by candles.

In Poland, however, there is a tradition that the cross on which Jesus died was made from a fir tree. The tree is said to have become an evergreen from the time when Jesus' blood was spilled onto the wood.

Christmas tree decorations

In ancient times fire and firelight were allied to the sun gods and this association was later linked to the power of Christ. At Christmas time it came to be linked, too, with the use of candles for decoration. Purpose-made candles for the decoration of Christmas trees probably came from the Erzebirge region of Germany where, in the early 1700s, instead of a tree a pyramid-shaped wooden framework was wrapped with greenery and decked with candles. The earliest Christmas tree ornaments were paper flowers, fruits and sweets; later, ribbons were used and then ornaments of glass or wax became popular.

Before long decorations for trees were being produced commercially and, again in Germany, glass baubles known as *kugeln* began to be popular. One town in particular became the centre for this new industry – Lauscha in the Thuringian mountain region of what was then known as Saxe-Coburg-Gotha.

In 1870, the technique of silvering the insides of the glass was introduced to make them appear more reflective in the candlelight. By the 1890s FW Woolworth began to make annual buying trips to Lauscha and in 1909 shop records show that he ordered some 216,000 ornaments from there. At the same time, manufacturers in the United States were also starting to produce tree ornaments so that by 1939 Corning Glass Works of New York had a machine that could produce two million ornaments each week.

Some facts about Christmas tree decorations

The idea for Christmas tree lights is thought to have come originally from Martin Luther, the German Protestant leader, in the 16th century. He was walking through a forest one Christmas Eve when he saw the lights from the stars above twinkling through the trees, so that they almost looked like lights on the trees themselves. To recreate this effect for his children, he took a small fir tree home with him and decorated it with candles.

Christmas-tree-lights were first mass produced in 1890, a few years after Edward Johnson (Thomas Edison's assistant) had come up with the idea for electric lights for Christmas trees. In 1909 the first electrically lit, decorated, public, outdoor Christmas tree was erected in Pasadena, California. It was quickly followed in 1910 by a 60 ft (18m) tree in Madison Square Park in New York.

Old Christmas tree ornaments are now very collectable. In 1994 Christie's sold 17 tin plate Christmas tree candle-holders for £900.

In 19th century Germany tinsel garlands for trees were made from real silver.

The earliest commercially produced electric tree lights retailed in the 1890s in the United States for $12 for 26 plain, frosted and red lights

It was in 1856 that the White House had its first decorated Christmas tree, installed by President Franklin Pierce. The first one lit with electric lights was in 1895.

4

Father Christmas or Santa Claus

'Twas the night before Christmas,
when all through the house
Not a creature was stirring, not even a mouse;
The stockings were hung by the chimney with care,
In hopes that St Nicholas soon would be there.
(Clement Moore, 1822)

St Nicholas, Father Christmas, Santa – whatever you call him, the stories of a genial gentleman who visits houses all over the world on the Eve of Christmas go way back in time.

Many of our present associations with this gentleman can be traced to Norse mythology. The ancient Scandinavians had a belief that, at the stroke of midnight on the longest night of the year, the god Odin would visit every household in the land. He was a god of magic and healing and, in order to visit everyone to bring them goodwill, peace and plenty, he would travel through the skies on a magnificent eight-legged horse. Entry into the houses could have been a problem, but he solved this by always entering through the smoke-holes in the roof.

Apart from that eight-legged horse, it all sounds familiar. Apparently, when the Scandinavians converted to Christianity, the Christian Church didn't care for the story of an eight-legged horse at all – and so the people changed it to a team of reindeer but still held to the main thrust of the story. I'm not too sure that the Church was any happier with flying reindeer, but I think they are here to stay now.

Incidentally, we still celebrate this pagan god every week since another version of his name was Woden, and it's from this that we get the word *Wednesday*. Another name for Woden was *Jolnir* from where we get *Jol* or *Yule*.

As we've seen, Christian beliefs soon became interlinked with the old pagan midwinter traditions, and eventually the story of Odin flying through the sky was linked with the Christian saint, St Nicholas.

There are numerous accounts of the miracles effected by St Nicholas. One story describes how he saved three young girls from a fate worse than death. St Nicholas was walking through the town of Myra in Turkey one day when he heard the sound of the girls crying within their house. Their father was so poor that he was unable to find the money to pay for dowries, and without a dowry they would have no chance of marriage and would be forced to sell themselves on the streets or into slavery. That night, when everyone in the household was asleep, St Nicholas returned and threw three bags of money in through a window of the house; they landed in the girls' shoes sitting in front of the fireplace.

The following morning the girls awoke and found the money and realised that their futures were assured. They had no idea how the money had got there and assumed that it must have fallen down the chimney to land in their shoes. This is where our tradition of putting stockings by the fireplace to receive presents comes from, and in fact in many parts of the world children put out their shoes or clogs.

In parts of Europe St Nicholas's name was pronounced *Santa Nicholaus* and, over time, this became abbreviated to *Santa Claus*. This was the name by which he was known to Dutch settlers when they emigrated to New Amsterdam in North America, a city that we now know as New York. From there the stories about Santa Claus spread throughout the United States and the rest of the world, so that today most children seem to know him as Santa rather than Father Christmas.

And what does he look like? Until the early years of the 20th century Father Christmas came in many different guises. He could sometimes be dressed in red but he was just as likely to be pictured wearing brown, or black, or green, or even blue. I once spoke to a lady who, remembering her own childhood in the years just after the First World War, described how her Father Christmas always wore blue. St Nicholas himself is usually depicted wearing green, however, to symbolise the coming of spring.

So why does he now have such a standardised uniform – red trousers and jacket trimmed with white ermine, glossy black belt and boots, the whole outfit topped with what can only be described as a red nightcap also trimmed in white? It's all due to the power of advertising. In 1931 Coca-Cola produced an advertisement picturing Santa Claus wearing the kind of clothes I have just described, and suddenly this was the only way he could be pictured. The power of advertising, indeed!

Returning to St Nicholas himself, he was originally buried in a tomb in Myra in Turkey and this became a centre of pilgrimage for generations of people. Then in 1087 some sailors stole his coffin and took it with them to Bari in Italy where they built not only a magnificent shrine for him but also a new church dedicated to the saint. Since then there has been an annual commemoration on 9 May each year in honour of the saint – the date on which his remains arrived in the town in 1087.

Rules for modern Santas

A Code of Conduct was drawn up in a meeting of Santas from all over Britain in 2005. It was decided that the following rules should apply to all Santas:

1   No bad wigs.
2   Beards must be kept to the same length (six inches long).
3   No trainers.
4   Santa should be able to say *Hello* in ten different languages.
5   Santa should never run or jump and should always act in an appropriate manner.
6   Santa should never smell of alcohol.
7   Santa should always know what are the most popular presents on the market each Christmas.
8   Santa should know about his own history and where he comes from.
9   Santa should always know the names of all his reindeer.
10   Santa should never use bad language.

In some areas, new rules specify that Santa should never let children sit on his knee – a sad reflection on our modern times.

Some facts about Father Christmas, St Nicholas or Santa

There are more churches in the world named for St Nicholas than for any other person in the whole history of the Church.

According to an old Irish legend St Nicholas's body was brought to Ireland from Italy by Crusaders returning from the Holy Land. His grave is said to be in the churchyard of the ruined St Nicholas's Church in Newton Jerpoint in County Kilkenny.

In France Father Christmas is called *Père Noël*, in Germany he's called *Weihnachtsmann*, in Denmark his name is *Julemand* and in Switzerland it's *Samiklaus*. In Finland he is known as *Joulupukki* which means Christmas Goat because presents were once given to children in Finland by a horned figure reminiscent of the masked dancers of the Roman festival of *Kalends*.

Father Christmas is usually thought of as being helped by elves. But in many parts of the world he is accompanied by a less welcoming helper who comes along to punish any children who have been naughty. This helper has many names amongst them *Knecht Ruprecht*, *Krampus*, *Klausmanneken* and *Zwarte Piet*.

In Russia Grandfather Frost (*Ded Moroz*) leads the winter celebrations. He is a character from Russian folklore and is based on St Nicholas. He usually arrives by sledge on New Year's Eve.

Finland is now officially the home of Father Christmas. In 1927 the Finnish Broadcasting Company accounced that a three-peaked hill in Lapland called Korvantunturi was his home. The name Korvantunturi means the hill with ears and from here Father Christmas can listen to the wishes made by children all over the world. The hill actually sits astride Finland's border with Russia. Finland is, of course, also the natural territory of reindeer.

Children all around the world write letters to Father Christmas in early December. Spanish children, however, send their letters to Balthazar, one of the three wise men, and he then brings them gifts at Epiphany.

Clement Clark Moore who wrote *'Twas the Night before Christmas* was a professor whose main work was a two-volume tome entitled *A Compendious Lexicon of the Hebrew Language*.

The illustrator whose Coca-Cola depictions provided us with the modern definitive version of Santa was Haddon H Sundblom. He also did work for companies such as Colgate, Maxwell House and Proctor & Gamble.

A man called Father Christmas was buried in the churchyard in the village of Dedham, Essex, on 30 May 1564. His headstone, if he ever had one, has long since disappeared. However, another headstone in Bluntisham-cum-Earith, Cambridgeshire, recalls someone called Christmas Day who died in 1940.

There are eleven American cities called Santa Claus. There are also over 70 people in the United States called S Claus.

Santa's address is Santa, Reindeerland, SAN TA1. In Canada in 1994 the Post Office issued Santa a postcode of his own – it is HO HO HO.

It has been estimated that each Christmas Eve Santa has to take around 2,000 million presents to something like 842 million houses and would therefore need at least 214,200 reindeer to pull his sleigh. And in the course of his journey he would travel over 220 million miles. The US-Canadian military organisation, Norad, which normally uses its radar to provide the North Americans with warning of missile and air attacks, tracks Santa's path as he travels across the globe. There's even a special website so that we, too, can follow him on Christmas Eve. It is www.noradsanta.org. This tracking began in 1955 when the director of operations at Norad's predecessor, the Continental Air Defence Command (Conad) received a telephone call asking where Santa was.

The world's first Christmas grotto was in Lewis's Bon Marche Department Store in Liverpool in 1879. It was called *Christmas Fairyland*.

Santa's reindeer

The reindeer that pull Santa's sleigh are the only ones in the world that can fly – they eat magic corn before they go on their epic journey each year, and this corn increases their strength to an infinite amount!

It was Clement Moore in his poem, *A Visit from St Nicholas* (usually better known as *'Twas the Night before Christmas*) who first gave Santa's reindeer their names – Dasher, Dancer, Prancer, Vixen, Comet, Cupid, Donder and Blitzen. Incidentally, Donder is more commonly known as Donner these days, but it was the name Donder that Moore actually used in his poem. Donder and Donner both mean *thunder* in Dutch and German respectively while Blitzen means *lightning*.

Notice that there is no mention of Rudolph – he didn't arrive on the scene until 1939. He was created by Robert L May who had been asked to write a Christmas story to help advertise a chain of department stores in the United States. The company wanted to produce some Christmas colouring books, and May wrote a poem based closely on Hans Christian Andersen's *Tale of the Ugly Duckling* for this purpose.

By 1946 more than six million copies of the booklet had been given to children, after which they were produced commercially, and in 1948 a nine-minute cartoon film about Rudolph was made.

Incidentally, because he was an employee of the company when he first wrote the story, it was the company that owned the copyright, so May didn't receive any royalties for his creation. Some years later he was deeply in debt and finally succeeded in 1947 in regaining the copyright, after which his financial future was assured.

Robert L May, who wrote the original story of *Rudolph the Red-nosed Reindeer*, first used the names Rollo and Reginald before finally choosing Rudolph.

Clement Moore chose eight reindeer in his poem *'Twas the Night before Christmas* because of the eight-legged horse named Sleipnir which carried the Norse god Woden through the skies.

Santa's sleigh first appeared (with just one reindeer) in a children's book called *The Children's Friend: a New Year's Present to Little Ones Five to Twelve* by Washington Irving.

Some facts about reindeer

There are no reindeer living at the North Pole so Santa couldn't possibly live there. Instead he must live in Lapland.

Reindeer are the only deer in which both sexes have antlers. However, each winter the male reindeer lose their antlers and re-grow them in the spring, so the reindeer that pull Santa's sleigh must all therefore be female.

Reindeer are immensely strong and are able to pull twice their own weight on a sleigh. In winter their hooves change to become concave so that they can grip more easily when walking on ice.

A reindeer's coat is like a super-warm duvet. Each hair is hollow to give additional insulation. To help keep them warm reindeer also have hair from the tips of their noses to the balls of their feet.

Reindeer have specialised snouts to warm the air as they breathe in.

37% of Finnish Lapps rely on reindeer-breeding for their income. Their herds can have up to 1,000 animals in them.

5

Christmas presents and cards

And when they were come into the house,
they saw the young child with Mary his mother,
and fell down, and worshipped him:
and when they had opened their treasures,
they presented unto him gifts;
gold, and frankincense, and myrrh.
(Matthew, Chapter 2)

Giving gifts has been synonymous with Christmas since the very beginning. In fact it was already the custom among the Romans to exchange gifts at the celebration of *Saturnalia*. And, of course, the three kings presented the baby, Jesus, with their gifts of gold, frankincense and myrrh.

To early Christians, and indeed to the pagans before them, these three gifts were all highly symbolic. **Gold** obviously represented wealth, but here it also symbolised kingship – Jesus would, in the future, be hailed as the King of the Jews.

Frankincense is a resin that comes from small thorny trees that grow in countries around the Red Sea. Once it has oozed from the tree, the sap hardens to form yellow-coloured crystals and these, when burnt, give off a heady aroma. It was used in religious ceremonies in temples in ancient times and was highly prized. It was a particularly important commodity in Yemen where the Queen of Sheba is said to have lived; her wealth was based on trade in frankincense.

Because of its associations with temples, frankincense therefore symbolised the Deity of Christ.

Myrrh is another valuable and rare resin, and it was used like frankincense in temples. It had other uses too – in cosmetics and perfumes, for example, and in early medicines.

But there was another use for myrrh – it was used by the Egyptians in the process of embalming. By embalming bodies the Egyptians were, of course, ensuring that the dead would be able to return to live in an afterworld sometime in the future. To early Christians, therefore, the symbolism of myrrh was quite obvious: it was a reminder that, although Jesus had died on the Cross for mankind, He would eventually be raised from the dead to live for evermore.

Gifts have therefore long been associated with the Christmas season; however until the Victorian period they were usually exchanged on New Year's Eve. In feudal times it was normally gifts of food that were given, and many would have been given by the peasants to their landlords as a form of rent. Fortunately for the poorer people in society this was later changed so that gifts were given in Christmas boxes (usually containing money) by employers to their staff and servants.

In the 19th century a new commercialism ensured that gifts of all kinds were exchanged, and it wasn't long before shopkeepers saw the benefits to their trade and began to market goods simply as Christmas presents.

Some facts about gold, frankincense and myrrh

Gold is usually mixed with another metal to give it strength. The purity of gold is measured in carats – 24-carat gold is pure gold.

The richest goldfield in the world is at Witwatersrand in South Africa.

It isn't known when gold was first discovered, but it was being used for cups and jewellery in the Middle East by 3500 BC.

There are over 52 references to frankincense in the Bible.

Frankincense has been used in the treatment of asthma, snakebites, diphtheria, meningitis and syphilis.

Myrrh was used in the past as an antiseptic.

Today myrrh is used to produce medicines for the treatment of sore throats and infections such as athletes' foot and thrush.

According to a 6th century Armenian text the three kings brought with them rather more than just gold, frankincense and myrrh. Melchior brought myrrh and aloes, rare fabrics and ancient books. Caspar brought frankincense and also nard (an exquisite perfume) and cinnamon while Balthazar besides gold also brought silver, sapphires and pearls.
But there is confusion here too. Some texts say it was Melchior who brought the gold, Caspar who brought the myrrh and Balthazar who brought frankincense.

In 1914 Christmas boxes were given to all members of the armed forces. These gifts were the idea of Princess Mary, the 17-year-old daughter of King George V and Queen Mary. Some two and a half million were given out and each small, decorated brass tin contained tobacco and some cigarettes, a lighter, a pencil and a Christmas card with a photograph of the Princess inside. The cost of providing these boxes was funded largely by public donation with some £200,000 being raised.

The wrapping of Christmas gifts is thought to have originated in Denmark.

For early Christians it was Christ rather than either St Nicholas or Father Christmas, who brought their gifts. Sermons until as late as the 16th century can be found where specific reference is made to Christmas presents as *Christ-bundles*.

The Romans also exchanged gifts at their festival for the January *Kalends* (in other words at the new year). These gifts were called *strenae* and the word is still found in the French custom of exchanging New Year gifts called *étrennes*.

In the West Indies material gifts were not exchanged. Instead it became the custom to exchange hospitality or services – an idea that I think should be encouraged in our materialistic age.

Members of the royal family always exchange and open their presents on Christmas Eve. Then, on Christmas morning, they all wake up to find a stocking at the foot of their beds – I wonder who fills those?

Gift-wrapping paper was not rationed in the United Kingdom during the Second World War because the government believed that it raised morale. Sales of wrapping paper actually increased by more than 20% during the war.

Christmas cards

Today many of us abhor the commercialism of Christmas and associate the exchanging of Christmas cards with this trend, and indeed there is some truth in this. But there's more to cards than just a means of making a profit for those who produce them.

Although hand-drawn cards had been produced earlier, the first **printed** Christmas card was designed by JC Horsley for Sir Henry Cole. Cole was a businessman who lived in Bath, and he sent it to his grandmother in 1843. Fortunately for posterity, she was so delighted when she received her card that she kept it – in 2001 it was sold at auction for the sum of £20,000. It took the form of a 5" x 3" postcard and shows a Victorian family enjoying their Christmas dinner.

Henry Cole had 1,000 of the cards printed and the remaining 999 were sold for one shilling each (5p). When you consider that this was the equivalent of an average man's weekly wage at the time they were not cheap. Twelve of them are known to be still in existence.

The idea for Christmas cards took off quickly, but only amongst the wealthier element in society since some cards at this time could cost up to five guineas. Fortunately, before long, mass production of cheaper, printed cards brought prices down.

The mid 1800s were years that saw the development of an increasingly mobile population as more and more people moved from the country to seek work in the developing towns, or travelled from Britain to all corners of the globe. It was a period, too, that saw a growing middle class with spare cash to spend on things other than necessities. Christmas is a time, moreover, when families that are split up want to make a special effort to keep in touch so, when in the 1870s

56% of cat owners buy their cat a present at Christmas time whereas 70% of dog owners do the same. Altogether some £27 million is spent in Britain each year just on presents for pets.

a special cheaper rate was introduced for the postage of cards, it was inevitable that they should suddenly become popular with people of all classes, hence the commercialism that is so often associated with Christmas cards in particular. In fact it had become so popular that by 1880 the Post Office was already urging people to *Post Early for Christmas*.

Some facts about Christmas cards

Some early Christmas cards weren't sent at Christmas – in the 1790s it was already popular amongst some people to send each other Twelfth Night cards

Sir Henry Cole, who produced the first printed Christmas card, also invented the perforated postage stamp. Furthermore, he was closely involved with the arrangements for the Great Exhibtion in 1851 and later became Director of the Victoria and Albert Museum in London.

Just as Oscars are awarded to the best films each year so there are awards for the best-designed cards. These are known as *Henries*, in honour of Sir Henry Cole.

Queen Victoria sent her first Christmas cards in the 1840s. The Queen and Prince Philip now send around 850 cards each year whilst the average in Britain is for each of us to send 50 Christmas cards. Within the United Kingdom this means that some 740 million cards are posted every Christmas.

The poet, Alfred, Lord Tennyson, was once asked to write some verses for a Christmas card for a fee of 1,000 guineas – but he turned it down.

The world's most expensive Christmas card wasn't made of card, nor did it really celebrate Christmas. It was made from ivory decorated with 44 diamonds and showed scenes from the life of Budda – it was worth £500,000 when it was made in the early 1900s.

Austria was the first country to issue a special Christmas stamp, in 1937. The Canadians, however, will tell you they had the first Christmas stamp. Their stamp, though, was one that was first issued on Christmas day (in 1898) rather than a specifically designed Christmas stamp. Britain's first Christmas stamp didn't appear until 1966 following a competition for children to design the stamps. The winning stamps featured a king's head and a snowman.

In 1969 the Christmas Philatelic Club was formed, just for Christmas stamp collectors.

The world's biggest Christmas card was once painted on the side of a QANTAS Boeing 707. It read *Have a Qantastic Christmas*. The world's smallest Christmas card, on the other hand, was sent to the Prince of Wales in 1929 – inscribed on a single grain of rice. But I don't think either of them count as proper cards.

In 1871 the *Christmas Letter Mission* began in Brighton. This was founded by a group of ladies who decided to send Christmas cards (with letters enclosed) to anyone unlucky enough to be spending Christmas Day in hospital (in the county of Sussex, anyway). Within ten years this had become a national organisation sending letters to people in prisons and workhouses as well as to those in hospital. Around 300,000 such letters were then sent out each year – and they wouldn't have been typed or word-processed either!

Robins at Christmas

Have you ever wondered why it is that, of all the birds we see in our gardens, it should be the robin that has come to be especially associated with Christmas cards? When the new Penny Post service was introduced in 1840 postmen wore a uniform that included a bright red waistcoat, and before long they were nicknamed *robins*. So once Christmas cards became popular, it wasn't long before the human "robins" were delivering cards that pictured the birds.

There is also a delightful tale that gives robins a special significance at Christmas time: Mary was nursing Jesus in the stable in Bethlehem beside a small fire, when a little brown bird noticed that the fire was going out and that Mary and the baby would get chilled. So the little bird approached the fire and flapped its wings in order to get the fire going once more, but in the process it singed its tummy – and that is why the robin has a red breast.

Some facts about robins

Their Latin name is *Erithacus rubecula* and they are to be found over most of northern Europe. Although associated in our minds today with gardens, they are in fact a woodland species.

To the Saxons a robin was a *ruddoc*, a word that still survives in our language today as *ruddy*. By the Middle Ages it was known as a *redbreast*, and the name *robin* was only officially recognised for the breed as recently as 1952.

Unlike many species of bird, robins sing all year.

The red plumage acts as a warning to other birds – when it feels threatened, a robin will puff out its chest to make it appear as large as possible while giving its distinctive *tic-tic-tic* warning call.

Despite their attractive image on our Christmas cards, robins are very territorial and will aggressively defend their territory against other robins and birds in general. They are, however, monogamous and tend to pair up around Christmas. A pair will then raise three to five broods, each usually of six eggs, in the spring. Eggs are incubated for 14 days and then the fledglings fly off after three weeks.

6

A Puritan Christmas

The people of England do hate to be reformed ...
These poor simple creatures are mad after
superstitious festivals, after unholy holidays.
(A Puritan MP speaking to the
House of Commons in the 1600s)

The celebration of Christmas was banned by the Puritans.

The actual Act of Parliament that officially banned the celebrations was passed during the reign of Charles I in 1644, but by this time the King no longer had control over what decisions were made by Parliament. Then in 1647 another law was passed, and this went even further – no longer was there even to be a holiday at Christmas. By the same act a number of other holidays (*holy days*, and therefore considered to be Papist) were banned too.

In fact, the whole legal system at the time seems to have been in a terrible muddle. One law stated that Christmas Day was no longer to be a holiday and everyone had to work. Another insisted that Christmas Day was to be a day of fasting. Yet another law prohibited any *worldly labours or work of ordinary calling* on Sundays or fast days. It would therefore appear that if you had a holiday on Christmas Day you were breaking the law but, at the same time, if you worked on a day of fasting (which Christmas now was) you were also breaking the law.

As it was a day of fasting, no food could be prepared on Christmas Day, and so special constables were given the power to enter people's homes in order to check up on this; any food that they found in the ovens they could confiscate. And all those pagan decorations? It became the task of London's Lord Mayor to go around the City removing any decorations that had been put up.

You weren't even allowed to celebrate Christmas with a special church service. However, it also became a criminal offence not to attend church on Christmas Day. And no matter where you lived, you had to walk to church; the use of any kind of transport was forbidden – in

fact if you went to church in a carriage, the constables had the right to confiscate this, sell it, and then give the proceeds to the poor.

What other changes did the Puritans make to Christmas? The singing of Christmas carols was banned for one thing. It also became illegal to eat Christmas pies (as mince pies were more commonly known). Even the throwing of snowballs was banned – this was described as *a profane pastime*.

Keeping within the law at Christmastime must have been extremely difficult in the mid-1600s. All the fun went out of Christmas – but, then, that was the Puritans for you!

The idea of banning Christmas had originated amongst the Presbyterians in Scotland, who felt strongly that Christmas was a pagan celebration and that there was no authority for it anywhere in the New Testament. As you can imagine, such thinking was unpopular throughout the rest of the country, so that, following the execution of Charles I in 1649, many people supported the return of his exiled son, the future Charles II, simply because he promised that he would restore Christmas, which is of course what happened.

After the accession of Charles II to the throne in 1660, all these laws were quietly forgotten. But they were never actually repealed so that, technically at least, it is still illegal to eat Christmas pies (for example)!

In Scotland, meantime, where puritanical ideas were more extreme, even the accession of Charles II couldn't persuade many Scots to bring back Christmas in its old form. Here, especially in the Lowland areas, the Puritans still held sway. In fact, well into the 20th century many Scots considered the English to be heathens because of the way they celebrated Christmas.

But the Scots like a good party just as much as the rest of us, and many of them still wanted to celebrate. So they got around it by holding their Christmas parties on New Year's Eve. Thus, no-one could accuse them of celebrating on Christmas Day itself. This is why it is that, ever since, the Scots have become famous for their Hogmanay parties.

For many people the idea of Christmas as an ordinary day of work persisted, and it wasn't until the Bank Holiday Acts in the 1870s that people in all walks of life could expect a holiday on that day. The holiday was then also extended to Boxing Day for staff in banks, public offices and stock exchanges. But it was only as recently as the 1950s that it became the norm for public services (such as trains) to be closed down for the holiday. In Scotland, however, Christmas Day remained an ordinary working day until 1958.

Following the banning of Christmas celebrations, riots broke out all over the country. At one time some ten thousand men in Kent rioted, saying that if they couldn't have their Christmas Day back, then they would rather have the King on the throne once more.

The mid-1600s was a time when pamphlets discussing all sorts of subjects began to be produced in great quantities. Christmas featured in many of them, and arguments were made on both sides of the debate.
The first page of one such pamphlet is titled:
The TRYAL of Old Father Christmas for Encouraging his MAJESTY'S Subjects in Idleness, Gluttony, Drunkenness, Gaming, Swearing, Rioting, and all Manner of Extravagance and Debauchery.

The Puritans, with their hatred of any form of jollification at Christmas time, took their ideas with them when they emigrated across the Atlantic. In 1659 in the state of Massachusetts the celebration of Christmas was made a crime there too. Although this law was repealed in 1681, five years later when the State Governor wanted to attend a service on Christmas Day he needed an escort of soldiers to ensure his safety. Some years after that, in 1706, a mob in Boston smashed the windows of a church because a service was being held there on Christmas Day.
Fortunately for all children in the United States today, in nearby New York (which had been founded by Dutch settlers rather than English Puritans) the people continued to celebrate Christmas, and it was from there that most ideas about Christmas celebrations spread around the new country.
But many people in New England continued to ignore the date right up to the late 1800s. It was only in 1870 that Christmas Day was finally declared to be a national holiday in the United States, since when the Americans have absorbed with gusto all the world's different ways of celebrating Christmas.

7

Christmas carols and music

I heard the bells on Christmas Day
Their old, familiar carols play,
And wild and sweet the words repeat
Of peace on earth, good-will to men!
(Henry Wadsworth Longfellow)

Carols predate Christmas – which seems a strange thing to say, but they were originally just songs that were sung during the Midwinter festivities. The word comes from the Greek *choros* meaning "a band of dancers and singers" and probably at first referred to songs more like our modern folk songs, which people could sing together and to which they would often dance.

For many centuries there was no religious element in them at all, and so it followed that for a long time the Church was extremely uneasy about them. The music of carols is wonderful toe-tapping stuff and it has often been said, after all, that the Devil has the best tunes. No wonder the Church was so worried.

Indeed, the Council at Avignon tried to ban carol singing as early as 1209, and again in the 15th century the Church was condemning the singing of carols. But they thrived and became particularly popular in this country in the 15th and 16th centuries.

And then the Puritans really did ban them. As was the case with the earlier Roman Catholic unease concerning carols, it was probably the reference to things that had strong pagan elements, such as holly and ivy, that made them so uncomfortable. So, in the 1640s, the singing of carols was prohibited by an Act of Parliament. In fact, so nervous were the authorities about this that anyone heard singing them was liable to be accused of witchcraft – this was especially the case in Scotland at the time.

With the Restoration of Charles II to the throne in 1660, the official prohibition on singing carols came to an end, but by then the damage had been done and many churches for years wouldn't allow carols to be sung within their doors.

Carols were therefore sung by groups of people outside their local churches. And this was why, in towns and villages up and down the country, a tradition of wandering from house to house singing carols developed.

It was only gradually, during the 18th century, that carols began to be received favourably by the Church. One of the earliest carols to be sung inside churches was *While shepherds watched their flocks by night*; the words of the carol were so close to those written in the Bible that it could hardly be seen as sacrilegious.

Slowly, others were allowed into the churches too – *Hark, the herald angels sing* was another that was being sung in churches in the 1700s. But well into the 20th century, there were still many carols that weren't considered suitable to be sung inside a church. *The holly and the ivy*, with its pagan symbolism, is an example.

Today, however, virtually all carols are sung in church and many new ones are constantly being added to the repertoire. Nor do many of these new ones fit our idea of what Christmas is traditionally all about – one recent carol portrays Mary as a teenage mother, whilst another, *Every star shall sing a carol,* has references to space travel.

In fact it could be said that carols are going back to their non-Christian beginnings and many of our traditional Christmas carols have recently been rewritten in such a way as to eliminate any reference to the religious aspects of Jesus, cribs or angels. Even gender references have sometimes been removed in an attempt to make the carols not only multi-faith but politically correct as well!

The traditional period in which to sing carols is from
21 December (St Thomas's Day) until the morning of
Christmas Day.

In many respects carol singing was a continuation of an old
tradition of *wassailing*, originally for the singing of all kinds
of songs. The term wassailing comes from the Old English
words, *Waes hael!* meaning *Be Healthy!* or *Good Health!* Carol
singing was thirsty work and people needed a drink (or several)
to keep going. Waes hael! was a toast that was made as you
took your drink.
In fact the word *toast* comes from this tradition too – the drink
would consist of a mixture of warmed ale with spices such as
nutmeg or ginger and sometimes honey was added. Into this
mixture small croutons or pieces of toast would be sprinkled.
How it came about that this gave rise to the term *to toast*, no-
one seems to know.

The twelve days of Christmas

This carol is thought to date from the 16th century, a time in Britain
of great religious upheaval. The century ended with the dominance
of the Protestant religion and with Roman Catholicism being driven
underground. Roman Catholics then, and for the subsequent two
centuries and more, were not allowed to practise their faith publicly
and so it is said that this carol was written to help the children of Roman
Catholics learn their Catechism. To those people not in the know it
would have appeared as simple rhyming nonsense, but to Roman
Catholics each of the verses had a secret meaning.

By a happy coincidence the Christmas holiday was celebrated
over a period of 12 days and so, too, was the Catechism divided into 12
parts. The *true love* who is sending all the gifts is not a human lover, of
course, but refers to God himself. *Me* – well that refers to those people
baptised into the true faith, Roman Catholicism in this case.

The meaning and symbolism behind the individual parts of the
carol are thought to be as follows:

On the first day of Christmas my true love sent to me
A partridge in a pear tree.
The partridge in a pear tree is a reference to Jesus Christ, the Son of
God. The tree is probably a reference to the cross on which Jesus was
crucified although it might also refer to the Tree of Knowledge in the
Garden of Eden. A hen partridge will sometimes feign injury in order
to act as a decoy when her nestlings are threatened, reminding us that
Jesus was prepared to die on the cross for all our sakes.

Two turtle doves
This is thought to refer to the two sections of the Bible, the Old and
New Testaments.

Three French hens

There's a great deal of disagreement as to what exactly this refers – is it the Trinity of God the Father, God the Son and God the Holy Ghost? Or is it the three virtues – Faith, Hope and Charity? Then some say, because this is after all a Christmas carol, that it refers to the three wise men who visited the infant Jesus. I think you can choose whichever works best for you.

Four calling birds

This, however, is almost certainly referring to the four gospels of Matthew, Mark, Luke and John. Instead of calling birds, some versions of this carol refer to *colly* birds. Colly (or collie) was an old English dialect word meaning *coal dust*, so in fact your true love would be sending you four blackbirds.

Five gold rings

This is another reference to books in the Bible, in this case to the first five books of the Old Testament (known as the *Pentateuch*). These books tell us the early history of man, as it was understood at the time the Bible was written. The books are Genesis, Exodus, Leviticus, Numbers and Deuteronomy.

Six geese a-laying

We are still with the Old Testament here. It's the words *a-laying* that give you a clue to the meaning – this is in fact a reference to the six days of the Creation.

Seven swans a-swimming

This refers to the Seven Gifts of the Holy Spirit mentioned in the Book of Romans. In other words, these are gifts given to us by God that we should use for the common good.

Having then gifts differing according to the grace that is given to us, whether prophesy,

RECIPE
TURTLE
DOVE
PIE

MY
TRUE
LOVE

If you count up all the presents given over the 12 days of Christmas in the carol, you end up with 364 gifts, one for each day of the year except Christmas Day itself.

let us prophecy according to the proportion of faith; or ministry, let us wait on our ministering; or he that teacheth on teaching; or he that exhorteth, on exhortation; he that giveth, let him do it with simplicity; he that ruleth, with diligence; he that showeth mercy, with cheerfulness.
(Romans, Chapter 12)

Eight maids a-milking
This is a reference to the Eight Beatitudes or, in other words, the blessings listed in Matthew's Gospel.
Blessed are the poor in spirit: for their's is the kingdom of heaven. Blessed are they that mourn: for they shall be comforted. Blessed are the meek, for they shall inherit the earth. Blessed are they which do hunger and thirst after righteousness: for they shall be filled. Blessed are the merciful: for they shall obtain mercy. Blessed are the pure in heart: for they shall see God. Blessed are the peacemakers: for they shall be called the children of God. Blessed are they which are persecuted for their righteousness' sake: for their's is the kingdom of heaven.
(Matthew, Chapter 5)

Nine ladies dancing
Sometimes thought to be a reference to the *nine choirs of angels,* this is more generally thought to mean the nine fruits of the spirit listed in Galatians.
But the fruit of the spirit is love, joy, peace, longsuffering, gentleness, goodness, faith, meekness, temperance: against such there is no law.
(Galations, Chapter 5)

Ten lords a-leaping
When you think of the number ten in the Bible you automatically think of the Ten Commandments and, sure enough, this is the case here.

Eleven pipers piping
This refers to Jesus' disciples. Yes, there were twelve, but this is a reference to the eleven of them that proved to be faithful to Jesus at the end.

Twelve drummers drumming
This brings us back to the reason for the carol in the first place – it's a reminder of the 12 points of belief that make up the Creed:

1	*I Believe in God the Father Almighty, Maker of heaven and earth;*
2	*And in Jesus Christ, his only begotten Son, our Lord.*
3	*Who was conceived by the Holy Ghost and born of the Virgin Mary;*
4	*Suffered under Pontius Pilate; He was crucified, dead and buried.*
5	*He descended into Hell; the third day He rose again from the dead;*
6	*He ascended into heaven and sitteth on the right hand of God, the Father Almighty.*

7	*From thence He shall come to judge the Quick and the Dead.*
8	*I Believe in the Holy Ghost, the holy catholic church,*
9	*The communion of saints,*
10	*The forgiveness of sins,*
11	*The resurrection of the body,*
12	*And the life ever lasting.*
	Amen.

Incidentally, every year someone, taking the words of the carol literally, tries to work out the cost of buying all of the above for one's true love. You are probably looking at spending something in the range of £35,000 to £40,000 at present rates.

Other favourite Christmas carols and songs

We had a very nice carol party here the other night –
we sang all REAL carols, no Wenceslases or Silent Nights.
(Ralph Vaughan Williams, the composer, in a letter dated 1956)

Many carols were collected and preserved by William Sandys, a solicitor and antiquarian. In 1833 he published *Christmas Carols Ancient and Modern* and this provides, for example, the earliest reference to *The First Noel*. Because many of the carols collected in the 19th century came from different sources, it is often difficult to be sure when some of them were first written and even where they came from. *The First Noel* is believed to have originated in the West Country, but otherwise little is known about it.

Perhaps the first carol most of us learn is *Away in a Manger*. This carol may be German in origin, going back to the time of Martin Luther – but we have no way of knowing for sure as it wasn't published until 1885. Another English carol that uses this theme and is certainly very old is *A Child this day is Born*, a version of which dates back to the early 1300s.

God Rest Ye Merry, Gentlemen is another old carol dating back, in this case, to the 1500s. Incidentally, notice where the comma should fall in this song – despite what most of us think when we sing it, this carol does not refer to merry (or drunk) gentlemen but, instead is wishing a merry (or happy) time to everyone. This is one of those carols that would never have been sung in church in the past, as was the case with *The Holly and the Ivy,* which dates from 1710.

Good Christian Men, Rejoice is thought to have originally been a German carol that was partly written in Latin (*In Dulci Jubilo*) and it could be some six or seven hundred years old. It was translated in the mid-1800s by John Mason Neale whose book, *Carols for Christmastide,* was published in 1853 and included the translations of a number of European carols.

Another of Neale's translations was *Good King Wenceslas,* the tune of which is thought to date back to the 1300s. The story concerns a duke (not a king) who lived in Bohemia and was born about 907 AD. Wenceslas became Duke at the age of 15 but was murdered by his

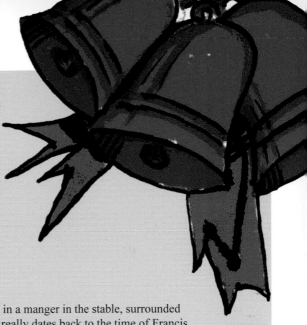

The service of nine lessons and carols that has become such an essential part of the religious festivities at Christmas began in 1878. The first service was held in Truro Cathedral and it then included two lessons with carols and also prayers and a sermon. A service similar to the present one was held in King's College Chapel in Cambridge in 1918, and it is from here that it is now broadcast every year.

The idea of the Baby lying in a manger in the stable, surrounded by animals, is an image that really dates back to the time of Francis of Assisi. In fact, so keen was he on promoting this particular image that he is the person credited with inventing the crib scene that is now a common feature of Christmas – or should be. Indeed, dancing and singing around a crib was already a part of Christmas festivities in Italy a century before St Francis, but he certainly popularised the idea.

brother when he was 26. He had worked hard to improve the lot of his people (presumably the thinking behind the words of the carol), and so he came to be venerated as a saint – he is now the patron saint of Bohemia. The Feast of Stephen, referred to in the carol, is the day after Christmas, Boxing Day. His own feast day is 28 September.

Another carol that was saved by being translated by Neale was *O come, O come, Emmanuel,* a Latin text that is thought to date back to the 12th century.

While Shepherds Watched Their Flocks By Night was written by Nahum Tate. He was Poet Laureate in the reign of Queen Anne so that this carol dates from about 1698 (although one reference gives a date of 1703). Because the wording is so similar to that in St Luke's Gospel, this was one of the first carols that was allowed to be sung in church.

And there were in the same country shepherds abiding in the field, keeping watch over their flock by night. And, lo, the angel of the Lord came upon them, and the glory of the Lord shone round about them; and they were sore afraid. And the angel said unto them, Fear not: for, behold, I bring you good tidings of great joy, which shall be to all people. For unto you is born this day in the city of David a Saviour, which is Christ the Lord. And this shall be a sign unto you; Ye shall find the babe wrapped in swaddling clothes, lying in a manger. And suddenly there was with the angel a multitude of the heavenly host praising God, and saying, Glory to God in the highest, and on earth peace, goodwill toward men.
(Luke, Chapter 2)

One of our most joyous carols, I always think, is *Hark! The Herald Angels Sing*, written by Charles Wesley in 1739 and it, too, was soon allowed in church. I don't think it would ever have been as successful a carol if he had stuck to his original words, *Hark! How all the welkin rings*, no matter how jolly the music. The word, *angel*, by the way, comes from a Greek word meaning *messenger*; in other words it could refer to anyone who passed on the news about the birth of Jesus.

Similarly, *We Three Kings of Orient Are*, were probably not kings at all, but wise men, astronomers most likely. Nor were there necessarily only three of them – we speak of that number because we know that they brought three gifts with them – but there could have been two, or several. Furthermore, it is not sexist to point out in this case that there could well have been women amongst them! This carol was written by Rev John Henry Hopkins in 1857.

Oh Come, All Ye Faithful (its Latin name is *Adeste Fideles*) was written in the early 1740s by John Wade. Wade was a fervent Jacobite and wrote a dedication at the start of the carol which reads *Regem nostrum Jacobum* (To James, our King), so many people have therefore come to see this as intended to rally Jacobite support in Britain at the time of Bonnie Prince Charlie's rebellion.

Joy To The World is another carol that dates from the 1700s. It was written by Isaac Watts and was based on the Ninety-eighth Psalm.

Make a joyful noise unto the Lord, all the earth: make a loud noise, and rejoice, and sing praise. Sing unto the Lord with the harp; with the harp, and the voice of a psalm. With trumpets and sound of cornet make a joyful noise before the Lord, the King.
(Psalm 98)

It Came Upon A Midnight Clear is an American carol written in 1849 by Edmund Sears who was a pastor in Massachusetts. Another American carol is *O Little Town of Bethlehem* which was written by a minister from Boston named Phillips Brooks in 1867. He was working at the time in Philadelphia and wanted a carol for the children in his Sunday School to sing.

The music for *Hark! The Herald Angels Sing* was composed by Mendelssohn and that for *In the Bleak Midwinter* by Gustav Holst.

How are three ships in *I Saw Three Ships* supposed to sail into Bethlehem on Christmas morning? The town is totally landlocked. In fact this carol has nothing to do with Christmas Day but, instead, originally referred to the journey taken by the relics of the three kings some 250 years later. Three ships (one for each of the kings) sailed through the Mediterranean, around Spain and France through the English Channel and up the River Rhine to the cathedral at Cologne where the skulls of the kings are said to be preserved to this day.

My turn of duty was from ten to twelve. I was standing there, gazing out, and I thought what a different Christmas this was going to be from any I'd ever had before. I thought that my family back home would be putting up their decorations as they always did after supper on Christmas Eve, and my father would be thinking about making his rum punch. I looked at my watch and at eleven I was standing there – it was exactly midnight by German time – and I suddenly saw lights appear in front of me all along the German trenches. I was wondering what was happening, and they started singing Stille Nacht – Silent Night. I'd not heard it before and I thought what a beautiful tune it was.
(A letter from a soldier on the Western Front)

But of all the carols throughout the world, the international favourite must be *Silent Night, Holy Night*. *Stille Nacht*, as it was originally known, was written in the village of Oberndorf, near Salzburg in Austria. The village priest had a problem – the organ in his church was broken and he needed a carol that could be sung to the accompaniment of a guitar instead. His assistant, Joseph Mohr, had written a poem two years earlier for the village children, and so he and his friend, Franz Gruber, set the poem to music, and it was then sung for the first time on Christmas Eve in 1818.

It was some years before it became really popular, but by the end of the 19th century it had been translated into many languages and had spread all around the world. Without doubt, the most moving rendition of *Silent Night* must have been when it was sung at midnight on Christmas Eve in 1914. Some German soldiers began to sing the hymn whilst sitting in their trenches. Within minutes their enemies, the British soldiers, were singing it too in their trenches on the other side of No Man's Land – a poignant reminder of how we are all brothers under the skin, even in the midst of war.

There are so many popular carols that it's difficult to include them all – *Ding dong merrily on High* is said to be a French carol that dates from the 16th century. From Wales comes *Deck the halls with boughs of holly.*

Once in Royal David's city was written by Cecil Frances Alexander. She was the wife of the Bishop of Derry and wrote a number of poems for children as well as two hymns that have certainly stood the test of time – *All things bright and beautiful* and *There is a green hill far away,* both of which she published in 1848 in her book, *Hymns for Little Children.*

A rather more famous poet, Christina Rossetti (sister of Dante Gabriel Rossetti, the artist) also added to our collection of well-loved carols when she wrote *In the Bleak Midwinter.*

It's not just carols that are associated with Christmas. For many people, attending a performance of Handel's *Messiah* is an essential part of their Christmas celebrations. Written in 1741 (in just 24 days!) the *Messiah* was originally conceived as music for Easter time and it was first performed in Dublin in April 1742. But by the late 1700s it was already becoming traditional for the oratorio to be performed during Advent.

In 2005 the BBC asked people to vote for their favourite Christmas carols. The top three were *In the Bleak Midwinter, Silent Night* and *Hark! The Herald Angels Sing.*

As for other, less sublime, Christmas songs, *Jingle Bells* was written by James Pierpoint in 1857 as, believe it or not, a song for children in his Boston Sunday School to sing at Thanksgiving. They then sang it again at Christmas time and it's been considered a Christmas song ever since.

Another favourite for small children is *Rudolph, the red-nosed reindeer.* Although the story was written in 1939 it wasn't until 1949 that the first song version was produced and was an immediate hit for Gene Autry, selling two million copies within a year. Another Gene Autry hit was *Frosty the Snowman*, recorded in 1950. It was also recorded in 1953 by Perry Como.

But the best-known of all secular Christmas songs must be *White Christmas* by Irving Berlin. It was written in 1942 and first came to public attention in the film *Holiday Inn*, starring Bing Crosby. The song was an instant hit, so much so that it was used again a few years later in another film which this time was called *White Christmas* and again starred Bing Crosby.

Christmas is a time for giving, and one Christmas song that was produced for just this purpose was Band Aid's *Do They Know It's Christmas?* in 1984. This was written by Bob Geldorf and Midge Ure and released to support the Ethiopian Relief Fund selling 50 million copies around the world. Other artists who took part in the project included Bananarama, Duran Duran, Paul McCartney, Sting and U2.

It has been estimated that approximately 350 million copies of *White Christmas* have been sold either on records or as sheet music.

The odds on England having a white Christmas are generally around 60-1. Even if it snows everywhere else in the country, it still isn't technically a white Christmas unless snow falls on the roof of the London Weather Centre on Christmas Day itself, so that, according to the Met Office, we are likely in this country to get a white Christmas only once in every ten years. England had seven white Christmases in the entire 20th century. Using the Met Office criteria, however, there were only two – in 1938 and in 1976.

It may not be Christmas music but it was on Christmas Day in 1896 that John Philip Sousa wrote his famous march, *The Stars and Stripes for Ever*, while on board the *SS Teutonic* sailing between Europe and America.

Besides *Do They Know It's Christmas?* in 1984 other festive chart toppers have included *Mary's Boy Child* by Harry Belafonte in 1957, *Merry Christmas Everybody* by Slade in 1973, *When a Child is Born* by Johnny Mathis in 1976 and *Mistletoe and Wine* by Cliff Richard in 1988.

It was Christmas Day in the workhouse…
(GR Sims, 1877)
It's not just songs that have awakened us to the plight of others less fortunate at Christmas. This poem denouncing Victorian attitudes and the treatment of the poor, elderly and infirm was instrumental in the introduction of the old age pension.

Because they are so well-known it is very easy to parody Christmas carols. One that has come in for a great deal of such treatment is *Hark! The Herald Angels Sing* which, during the time of the Abdication Crisis in 1936, was rewritten as Hark, the herald angels sing, Mrs Simpson's pinched our king. This carol has even been used as an advertising jingle:

> *Hark! The herald angels sing,*
> *Beecham's pills are quite the thing,*
> *Two for a woman, one for a child,*
> *Peace on earth and mercy mild.*

or another version:

> *Hark! The herald angels sing,*
> *Beecham's Pills are just the thing.*
> *For headache strong, for stomach mild,*
> *Two for an adult, one for a child.*

We Three Kings has come in for similar treatment with:

> *We three kings of Leicester Square*
> *Selling ladies underwear*
> *How fantastic, no elastic,*
> *Only a penny a pair.*

and very popular in the 1960s was:

> *We four lads of Liverpool are,*
> *John in a taxi, Paul in a car,*
> *George on a scooter honking his hooter*
> *Following Ringo Starr.*

8
Christmas food

Christmas comes but once a year,
And when it comes, it brings good cheer,
Roast beef, plum pudding, strong ale and mince pie,
Who likes that better than I?

In the weeks following harvest time in the autumn, food would be plentiful. But, in the centuries before refrigeration or the canning of food became the norm, there were many kinds of food that would only last for a short time before going bad. So people tended to gorge themselves on those foods that were just about to turn rancid while they could still eat them at all.

This would have happened near the time of the winter solstice, and so gorging ourselves and feasting at this time of year goes back to the Stone Age.

Once food began to turn bad, it would be cooked with herbs and spices to try and disguise the fact that it was off. Home-grown herbs were cheap enough, but spices were extremely expensive as they

The original version of the above poem was:

At Christmas play and make good cheer,
For Christmas comes but once a year.

It was written in the 1500s by Thomas Tusser in a volume called *Five Hundred Points of Good Husbandry*. Tusser was also the person who coined the phrase *a fool and his money are soon parted.* Another version of the rhyme, dating from the 17th century, reads:

Now thrice welcome, Christmas,
Which brings us good cheer,
Minced pies and plum porridge
Good ale and strong beer.

had to be imported from distant lands. This meant that, for those people who could afford it, the use of lots of spices in food at such a time was an effective way of showing off one's wealth – which explains why we associate rich, highly spiced food with all the festivities of Christmas.

So, as you sit heavily in your chair on Christmas afternoon, regretting the fact that you've just eaten one mince pie or chocolate too many, you are quite simply continuing a tradition that goes way back in time.

To tell the truth, if you've eaten even one **mince pie** you will have broken the law. It seems incredible to think that Parliament, in the 1600s, could have passed a law banning the eating of Christmas pies, as they were then known! And since it has never been repealed we are each of us breaking the law every time we eat one.

You see, Christmas pies didn't always look quite as they do today. Originally they were oval in shape to represent the manger that Jesus was laid in after His birth. Inside the pastry "manger" went the mincemeat, and then on the top was placed a small pastry model of the baby in His swaddling clothes.

Puritans, however, were appalled by this representation of Jesus in a form in which He could be eaten. They called Christmas pies *abominable and idolatrous confections* and banned them.

It is bad luck to refuse to eat the first mince pie you are offered over the Christmas season.

But, of course, people liked eating them. So they changed the shape and made them circular. They continued to put the mincemeat inside, but on top, instead of having a pastry model of Jesus they rolled it out and used it as a cover. And then they changed the name and called them mince pies instead of Christmas pies – and continued to eat them!

Incidentally, the mincemeat that goes inside mince pies was at first made literally from minced meat and suet mixed with dried fruits. Over the years this has changed to become the sweeter mixture that we are all familiar with today and the meat content has completely vanished.

And, finally, you should always try to eat at least 12 mince pies over the Christmas holiday period, and each one should have been made by a different person and be eaten in a different house – this guarantees good luck over the coming 12 months.

A 1648 recipe for mincemeat published in a book called *The English
Huswife* included the following ingredients: 1 lb minced beef, lamb or
veal, 6 oz suet, 4 oz each of currants, raisins and prunes, some orange
peel, ground cloves and mace, sugar and salt and pepper. Notice that
mincemeat in those days actually had meat in it!

Mince pies are supposed to have three spices in them: cinnamon,
cloves and nutmeg. These represent the three gifts given by the Magi.

How delicious it smells! How round it is! A kiss is round,
the horizon is round, the earth is round, the moon is round,
the sun and stars, and all the host of heaven are round.
So is plum pudding.
(Illustrated London News, 1848)

Our traditional **Christmas pudding** at first had more of a porridge-like consistency and was known as *frumenty*. This was a fasting dish made from hulled wheat, boiled in milk with spices and sugar. Later minced beef or mutton and various dried fruits were added. By the 19th century it had become the solidified pudding that we now know, without meat, but with the addition instead of breadcrumbs and eggs. It was then known as **plum pudding** because of the prunes that were also used. One Christmas carol refers to it as *Figgy pudding*, figs being used in the recipe as well as prunes in this case.

Today a Christmas pudding is usually the shape of a pudding bowl, but if you look at Victorian scenes of families eating their Christmas dinner, you will see that the pudding is always shaped like a ball – this is because, in those days, the mixture was rolled up in a muslin cloth and moulded into shape before being suspended in a pan of boiling water. The pudding only became associated with Christmas when Queen Victoria's husband, Prince Albert, especially asked for it to be part of the Christmas dinner menu because he was particularly fond of such heavy, rich puddings.

Traditionally, the Christmas pudding was made on the last Sunday before Advent – *Stir Up Sunday* – and every member of the household would take a turn at stirring the mixture and making a wish while doing so. You should stir the pudding from east to west in honour of the Magi who travelled in that direction. The name *Stir Up Sunday*, however, has nothing at all to do with stirring puddings; instead it comes from the first words of the Collect that would be read out in church that day: *Stir up, we beseech Thee, O Lord, the wills of thy faithful people.*

During the Victorian period it also became the custom, when making Christmas puddings, to try and ensure that the ingredients used came from all around the British Empire, as it was then known. These included: flour from Canada, raisins from South Africa, sultanas and currents from Australia, sugar from Demerara (now part of Guyana), beef-suet from Scotland, eggs and cooking apples from England, spices from India, rum from Jamaica and brandy from Cyprus.

Plum puddings have been part of the Christmas festivities all around the world. Mary Seacole, nursing soldiers during the Crimean War in the 1850s, wrote of the puddings she and her fellow nurses made: *I fancy if returns could be got of the flour, plums, currants and eggs consumed on Christmas Day in the Crimean peninsula they would astonish us.*
Some years later Captain Scott and members of his expedition to the South Pole had Christmas pudding in 1911. And then, in 1916, 2.5 million pounds of pudding, on their way to British troops serving around the Mediterranean Sea, were lost when the ship carrying them was torpedoed off Malta.

*...like a speckled cannon-ball, so hard and firm, blazing in
half of half-a-quartern of ignited brandy, and bedight with
a Christmas holly stuck into the top.*
(A description of the Christmas pudding made by Mrs Cratchit
in Charles Dickens's *A Christmas Carol*.)

A recipe for Christmas pudding that appeared in 1861 in *Mrs Beeton's Book
of Household Management* included the following ingredients: 1½ lbs
raisins, ½ lb currants, ½ lb mixed peel, ¾ lb of breadcrumbs, ¾ lb of suet, 8
eggs and 1 wineglass of brandy. I wonder how many people it was expected
to feed?

Traditionally Christmas puddings should be made from 13 ingredients
altogether – to represent Jesus and the 12 apostles. But, of course, 13 is an
unlucky number and so a charm would be added to change any possible bad
luck into good. Charms in the pudding should include a coin (for worldly
fortune), a ring (for marriage) and a thimble (for a life of blessedness).

In the days of the Gold Rush in Australia people even baked Christmas
puddings with gold nuggets in the middle instead of charms.

It has been suggested that when we pour brandy over our Christmas
puddings and set them alight we are recalling a time when our ancestors
worshipped fire.

To encourage shoppers in the UK to buy ingredients from around the Empire
for their Christmas pudding, the town of Morecambe, in Lancashire, made
the world's largest Empire Christmas pudding in 1931. The pudding weighed
half a ton and took 60 hours to cook.

I didn't like the turkey, but I liked the bread it ate.
(A three-year old's comment after eating Christmas dinner)

Some facts about turkeys

The Mexican word for a turkey was *uexolotl*. It's said that turkeys were so-called because their heads were thought to resemble the head-dresses of Turkish men in the 1500s. In France, however, turkeys were introduced by Jesuits so that, in some parts of that country, they came to be known as *Jesuites,* but in the country of Turkey a turkey is known as a *hindi*.

The first turkeys were introduced to Britain by a Yorkshireman, William Strickland, who is said to have been a cabin boy on John Cabot's ship. He acquired them from some American Indians and subsequently sold them in Bristol for tuppence each. That was in 1526. He ended up making his fortune from this trade and later became Sir William Strickland with a turkey on his coat of arms.

George II so enjoyed eating turkey that he reared 3,000 of them in Richmond for his guests to eat.

The man who holds the record for plucking turkey is Vincent Pilkington of Ireland. He plucked 100 birds in just seven hours and 32 minutes in 1978.

The great 18th century American statesman and scientist, Benjamin Franklin, wanted to have the turkey as the national emblem of the United States. However, it was the Bald Eagle that was chosen instead. Somehow I think the right decision was made – a gobbling turkey doesn't quite have the same gravitas as an eagle.

Despite the fact that it was the month of July and not Christmas, the first meal eaten on the moon by Neil Armstrong and Buzz Aldrin was roast turkey.

American Indians used the spurs on the legs of male turkeys as projectiles on arrowheads.

93% of the population of the United Kingdom eats turkey on Christmas Day.

It was a Turkey! He never could have stood upon his legs,
that bird. He would have snapped 'em short off in a minute,
like sticks of sealing-wax.
(The description of the turkey bought by Ebenezer Scrooge
for the Cratchit family in *A Christmas Carol*)

But before you have your pudding and mince pies, you should really
eat the main course of your Christmas dinner – **turkey** or **goose**. Before
the introduction of turkey the most prized birds for your Christmas
dinner were bustard, goose, capon, peacock and, especially prized,
mute swan. Roast goose became the traditional bird during Elizabethan
times, especially amongst poorer families. Thus, the tradition began
whereby people would buy their goose in September or October (at
Nottingham's famous Goose Fair, for example) and fatten it up over
the following months in good time for the festivities. Even after it was
introduced to England it was some years before turkey took over as the
main meat at Christmas. For one thing, goose was cheaper than turkey
– perhaps because the meat was tougher.

Turkeys came from America and were first introduced into
Europe by Spanish conquistadors returning from there at the beginning
of the 16th century. Henry VIII was one of the first people in Europe to
have turkey for his Christmas dinner – apparently, in so doing, he was
breaking a tradition that the monarch had a swan at Christmas.

After being introduced from America, turkeys were reared in
Norfolk, and from here they had to travel to market in London. In the
days before modern transport systems the birds had to walk all the way

there – 100 miles – so that, in order to ensure that they could walk such a long distance, the farmers would make little boots for them from sacking or even leather. Geese also had to walk to market but, as they would just bite off their sacking boots, their feet were instead dipped in tar to protect them on the journey.

It's said that in Britain on Christmas Day we consume more than 10 million turkeys weighing 19,000 tons; 120,000 tons of potatoes; 15,000 tons of sprouts; 7.5 million carrots; 1,200 tons of parsnips; 1,600 tons of chestnuts; 5.2 million jars of cranberry sauce; 16 million packets of stuffing. This is followed by 12 million Christmas puddings; 250 million mince pies; 11 million Christmas cakes. Not to mention 40,000 tons of clementines, mandarins and satsumas.

For Christmas in 1213 the royal household consumed some 200 pigs, 1,000 hens, 15,000 herring, 10,000 salt eels, 100 lbs almonds, 50 lbs pepper and 27 hogsheads of wine. (A hogshead was a large cask capable of holding around 60 gallons.)

In order to burn off his gargantuan Christmas dinner, the average man would need to go for an 18 mile walk.

Few poor people had kitchens with ovens capable of roasting large joints of meat. Consequently, bakers would keep their ovens fired up after they had finished baking their bread so that such people could take their dinner to be cooked in the bakers' ovens. In *A Christmas Carol*, for example, this is how the Cratchitt family get their dinner cooked.

By the 19th century many people would save for their Christmas goose by joining a Goose Club, paying in 3d or 6d to the club each week. Unfortunately, many such clubs cheated their members (people who, of course, could least afford it) so that the Temperance League, among others, was very much against them.

Captain James Cook probably had the first Christmas dinner in Australia in 1769.

To wash down all that food you will need something to drink and the best known Christmas drink is probably a **punch**. Its name comes from the Hindu word *panch* meaning *five* (a reference to the five ingredients used in the early recipes) and was probably brought to this country from India by sailors and those who worked for the East India Company.

The first recorded reference to it dates back to 1632. At that time most punches had a wine or brandy base but sometime in the mid 1600s the modern punch was born with the introduction of Jamaican rum as a key ingredient. As early as 1671 there are references to *punch houses* where you could drink punch, as opposed to alehouses where only ale was available. Today, of course, a good punch seldom has just five ingredients and it isn't necessarily an alcoholic drink either.

Having had your Christmas dinner and pulled all your crackers, eaten some illegal mince pies and had far too much to drink, you might still wish to have a slice of **Christmas cake**. In the past these cakes were associated with the last night of the festivities – Twelfth Night. This was your last chance to have a party with fun and games and to feast before the season of jollification came to an end.

The Commander in Chief of the English navy in 1599, Sir Edward Kennel, made a huge punch on his ship on one occasion. He used 80 casks of brandy, 9 casks of water, 2,500 limes, 80 pints of lemon juice, 1,300 lbs of sugar, 5 lbs of nutmeg and 300 biscuits together with a large cask of Malaga wine. This was served by the ship's boys from a vast marble bowl to some 6,000 guests. Apparently, the fumes were so strong that the boys had to be replaced every 15 minutes.

Some facts about crackers

The first Christmas crackers went on sale in London in 1847.

By the end of the 1800s Tom Smith's company was already producing more than 100 different cracker designs.

A Royal Warrant was granted to Tom Smith's company in 1906 by the then Prince of Wales. This tradition continues today as both the Queen and Prince Charles have granted royal warrants to the company.

The company supported the suffragette movement by allowing special verses demanding votes for women to be put in some of their crackers.

During the Second World War cracker snaps attached to pieces of string were used to mimic the sound of gunfire when soldiers were undergoing training.

Approximately 130 million crackers are pulled each Christmas.

In 1927 a man sent the company an engagement ring (and ten shillings to cover any costs) for a special cracker to be made so that he could use it to propose to his girlfriend. Sadly he forgot to send his name and address, so the engagement ring and his note are still with Tom Smith's to this day.

Many of the original Victorian designs for Tom Smith crackers were lost when the factory was destroyed in the Blitz in 1941.

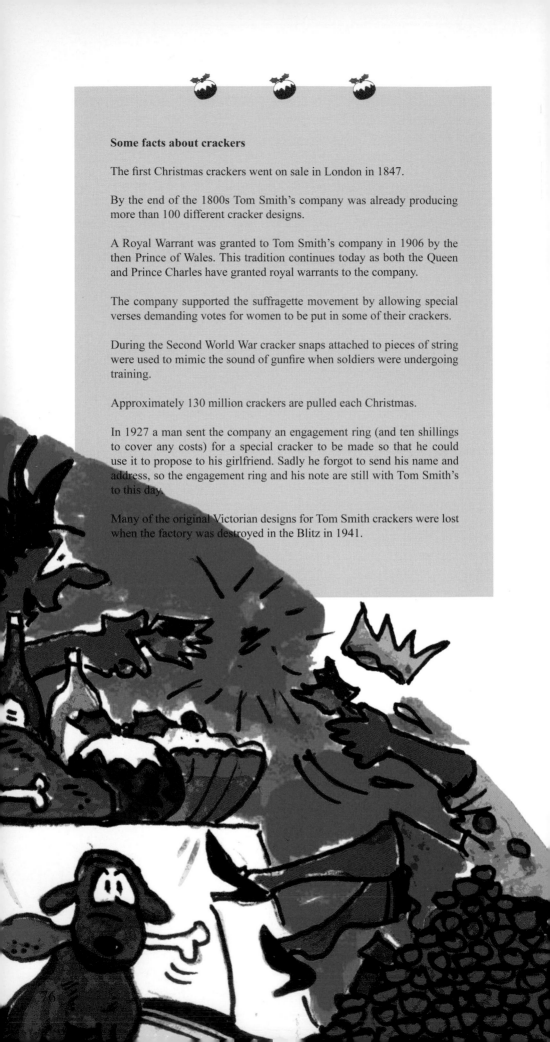

Christmas crackers

No Christmas table is complete without **crackers** for everyone to pull. These were the invention of a London baker called Tom Smith in 1846. In 1840 Smith visited Paris, where he was much taken with the tradition there of wrapping sugared almonds in a twist of paper (*bonbons*). He started selling these in London, and then realised that many of his customers were young men buying them as gifts for their sweethearts – and so he started placing little love mottoes within the wrappings. These were so successful that he had to increase his staff to help meet the demand.

One day he was sitting in front of his fire, when he noticed how delighted his children were each time the logs sparked and, in what can only be described as a flash of inspiration, he wondered if it would be possible to replicate the noise when people opened his bonbons. He experimented, burning his hands and his furniture in the process, and eventually cracked it, if you'll forgive the pun. By pasting saltpetre on two strips of thin card, he caused a *crack* to sound when they were pulled apart.

And so the Christmas cracker was born – except that in those days it was called a *cosaque*. The word came from *Cossack* because the sound of the crack was said to resemble the noise made when a Cossack soldier cracked his whip.

Tom Smith's idea was so popular that other people quickly tried to copy it and he rapidly had to take out a patent and form the company that still supplies crackers to this day.

Are these the best - or the worst - cracker jokes?

What's worse than a giraffe with a sore throat?
A centipede with sore feet.

What do you call a penguin in the Sahara Desert?
Lost.

What did the beaver say to the tree?
Nice gnawing you.

How does Jack Frost get to work?
By icicle.

What school subjects are snakes best at?
Hisstory.

What would you get if all the cars in Britain were red?
A red carnation.

Why do birds fly south in winter?
Because it's too far to walk.

Why did the star twinkle?
Because it saw the moonbeam.

How did Good King Wenceslas like his pizzas?
Deep pan, crisp and even.

What do you call a parrot with an umbrella?
Polly unsaturated.

How do you start a milk pudding race?
Sago.

What do you call a one-eyed dinosaur?
Do you think he saw us.

What lies in a pram and wobbles?
A jelly baby.

What lies at the bottom of the sea and shivers?
A nervous wreck.

Christmas food from other countries

Just as in Britain Christmas is associated with mince pies, so other countries have special foods that are linked to the festivities. In **Belgium**, for example, you will find Christmas trees that are decorated with spicy biscuits called *speculoos*. These were special treats for St Nicholas's Day. Similar cakes in **Germany** are called *lebkuchen*. Lebkuchen originated as honey cakes and are specially associated with Nuremberg where there is documentary evidence of a bakery that was producing them as long ago as 1395. They originated in monasteries in the area and were at first distributed by the monks to the local people. *Leb* means *healing* and these biscuits were thought to have medicinal properties.

In **Norway** and **Sweden**, your Christmas dinner will often include a rice pudding called *julgröt* although for some people this is a Christmas Eve supper dish. Like our Christmas pudding with its charms, this will have a single almond hidden in it and whoever gets the almond is guaranteed good luck for the coming year.

Cakes are always popular, particularly at Christmas and many countries have a special cake that is associated with the festivities. In **Germany** *Christollen* is a rich fruit loaf that was first made in about the 14th century and was baked in the shape of a baby in swaddling bands. Christollen was often eaten during Advent and so, since this was also a period of fasting, butter was deemed to be too rich and oil was used instead. Eventually, in 1490, the Elector of Saxony made a special request to the Pope that this "butter prohibition" should be lifted. However, the Pope then introduced a fine to be paid by those using butter in the recipe – this money was used to build Freiburg Cathedral.

In **France** the favoured Christmas cake is the *büche de Noël*, made to resemble a Christmas log. The Belgians do the same, but they sometimes place a fondant baby on the top of their log cakes.

On Christmas Eve the **Greeks** bake a sweet bread with dried fruits and spices called a *Christopomo*, literally, *Christ's bread*. They also have a sponge cake called a *vasilopeta* that is usually made on the last day of the year and then sliced and served right after the stroke of midnight. The first three slices cut from this cake are offered to St Basil, Christ and the Virgin Mary. Like our Christmas pudding this, too, will often have a silver coin hidden inside it.

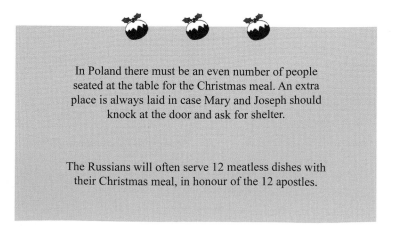

In Poland there must be an even number of people seated at the table for the Christmas meal. An extra place is always laid in case Mary and Joseph should knock at the door and ask for shelter.

The Russians will often serve 12 meatless dishes with their Christmas meal, in honour of the 12 apostles.

In Yorkshire it used to be traditional custom to serve a slice of Wensleydale cheese with Christmas cake.

In Sweden and Finland instead of turkey people sit down to ham for their Christmas dinner, while in Norway they have pork and dried cod. The Spanish often choose sucking pig, while the Dutch and Belgians prefer roast hare or game.

In America in the 19th century Christmas was known amongst the American Indians as the Big Eating, which seems entirely appropriate.

In Argentina there is a special Christmas food shaped so that it resembles babies wrapped in swaddling bands. *Niños envueltos* (which means *wrapped children*) are rolled slices of beef filled with mincemeat.

In **Italy** the traditional Christmas dish is a *panettone*, a type of cake that originated in Milan. Today's panettone is very different from the earlier versions – they used to be made from pasta that was not completely cooked and they also contained dry grapes that were left to ferment before the cake was eaten. Recent EU regulations about the thorough cooking of food mean that this is no longer allowed in its original form so that the panettone you eat today has totally changed from the traditional version. These days, too, you will often find chocolate, almonds or even ice-cream inside your panettone.

Yet other doughy, or bread-like, Christmas dishes (nearly all of them with dried fruits and spices in the recipes) include **Norway's** *Julekake*, *Beigli* pastry rolls filled with walnut or poppy seeds from **Hungary** and pastries called *turtes* in **Romania**. In **Czechoslovakia** they have a braided white Christmas bread called *calta* which is always eaten along with another special Christmas dish, a fruit stew known as *masika*.

9

Christmas entertainment

A Christmas family party! We know
nothing more delightful.
(Charles Dickens, *Sketches by Boz*)

In times past the period leading up to Christmas was generally a time of fasting and reflection and then Christ's birth was, of course, celebrated with a great feast on Christmas Day itself. It was after Christmas that people really started to enjoy themselves, often culminating in a particularly riotous party on Twelfth Night.

Stage plays and pantomimes

He's behind you!

The entertainment at these parties varied but amongst the most popular was the staging of plays. At first these were what are known as *mystery plays* and *mummers plays*. The two should not be confused – mystery plays are the earliest and their origin is obscure. They date from early medieval times and were generally re-enactments of Bible stories, usually produced by trade guilds within a town. As they became more popular, travelling companies of players began to take them over. These plays could be performed at any time of year, however, and many were associated with Easter. However, those that were performed at Christmas often had a strong element of the nativity story about them and could perhaps be described as the forerunners of the nativity plays that we watch each Christmas in primary schools up and down the country.

Mummers plays, on the other hand, weren't necessarily biblical. Developing also in medieval times, these plays tended to be more comic and many were associated specifically with Christmas. No-one seems to be sure where the word mummer has come from. Some say it's from a Middle English word *mum* meaning *silent* but since the plays weren't silent this seems unlikely. A more likely suggestion is that it either comes from the Greek *mommo* meaning *mask* or the German *mummer* which, similarly, means *to wrap up* or *disguise* and since many of the characters in these plays were masked or occasionally blacked their faces this derivation seems probable.

Meantime, another tradition was developing in Europe, perhaps from the mumming plays – the Italian *Commedia dell-arte* – and it was from this tradition that today's popular *pantomimes* derived in 18th century England so that many families now see going to a pantomime as an essential part of their Christmas festivities. At first pantomimes were short *mimed* interludes within much longer plays. As the ridiculous farces that we now watch, they reached the height of their popularity in Victorian times, and it was then that they came to be associated so closely with Christmas.

It was also during the Victorian period that the tradition of having a girl play the part of the principal boy, and men playing the part of old women developed, probably an example of the many topsy-turvy traditions associated with Twelfth Night.

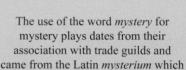

The use of the word *mystery* for mystery plays dates from their association with trade guilds and came from the Latin *mysterium* which means *handicrafts* – in other words a reference to the skills of the guild members who performed in them.

The first English pantomime was performed on 26 December 1717. In a pantomime in 1721 there was a reference to the financial scandal known as the South Sea Bubble, thus starting a tradition of making topical (often political) references during the show.

Father Christmas was a regular character in old mummers' plays which would be performed at Christmas time. The poet and playwright, Ben Jonson, had a Father Christmas character in *A Christmas Masque* which he wrote for King James I's court in 1625. In this play Father Christmas has a long beard and carries a thick club. He's also supported by children named Misrule, Minced Pie, Carol, Gambol, Post and Pair, New Year's Gift, Mumming, Wassail and Baby Cake.

Each year supermarkets all over the country prepare for a sudden surge in the sale of tea-towels as mothers of young shepherds buy them for their children to wear in school nativity plays. It's even known in some stores as the *Bethlehem boost*.

This is also a time when there is a boost in the sales of quilted toilet rolls – it seems people want to impress their guests at Christmas.

Rules for parents attending nativity plays

1. Don't ever offer to provide a genuine baby – it will either be dropped by Mary or spend the entire time screaming it's head off.
2. Don't bribe your children to behave when on the stage. They won't – but that's part of the charm of such plays.
3. If your son is one of the shepherd's don't give him a staff, he'll only use it as a sword or a gun.
4. If your son is a shepherd do get him a clean tea-towel to wear as a headdress.
5. Don't complain if your child is the back end of a donkey – you'll only provide the other parents with amusement.
6. If your daughter is Mary don't assume she's the star – teachers consider it a sit-and-do-nothing role for girls who have no acting ability whatsoever.
7. Don't embarrass your child by blubbing.
8. Ignore any rules that say you can't take your camera along. Despite what the school may say these rules have nothing to do with protecting the children from paedophiles but are there so that the school can subsequently profit by later selling you, at an exorbitant rate, their own film of the production.

And finally, do be glad that the primary school is having a nativity play at all – it's about the only time the children will ever learn about the true meaning of Christmas!

The Arabian geographer, Georg Jakob, writing in the 10th century, described eyewitness accounts that on the night of Christ's birth, despite the wintry weather, all the forest trees flowered and fruited. This magical moment was later woven into the Coventry mystery play, *The Birth of Christ*. Of course if Jesus was born in spring, as I suggest in Chapter 1, then the trees would be beginning to flower anyway, and it's certainly not unknown for bad weather with snows to fall in springtime, hence the reference to wintry weather in this account.

Christmas games

Today we tend to think of our Victorian ancestors as being very straight-laced and possibly quite incapable of being able to have a good time. Nothing could be further from the truth and it is when you start to look at the parlour games they would have played at Christmas time that this quickly becomes apparent.

One popular game in the 19th century was Snapdragon – a decidedly dangerous game too. A pile of raisins would be placed in a bowl of brandy, the lights would be turned out and the brandy set ablaze. You then had to grab the raisins to eat them and whoever ate the most without getting fingers or tongue burnt won the game. The trick was that you had to close your mouth on the burning raisin in order to extinguish the flame. Health and safety obviously was not a priority and many people got seriously burnt. In one case, in 1891, 15 children in Leeds were set on fire while playing this game and 11 of them later died.

Many Victorian games involved the payment of forfeits when people lost a game or made a mistake and it's amusing to see just how many forfeits had a decidedly sexual side to them. In one forfeit for example, gentlemen were blindfolded and had to go around the room kissing all the ladies. Hardly a forfeit you would think except that, as soon as he had been blindfolded, everyone present switched places so that the man paying the forfeit often found himself kissing all the men instead. In a similar forfeit, young girls were told they had to kiss each corner of the room but immediately the forfeit had been given, and before they had a chance to pay, suddenly there was a man stationed in each corner waiting to catch the kiss.

It's easy to see how simple parlour games soon became boisterous and perhaps it's not such a large step to go from there to the office parties of today, so that it is now said that over 90% of office Christmas parties are followed by at least one complaint of sexual harassment.

So many office workers have photocopied their bare bottoms at office parties that one manufacturer, Canon, has increased the strength of the glass in its machines to prevent accidents.

William Shakespeare wrote his play, *Twelfth Night*, for a court celebration on Twelfth Night in 1601. Indeed many elements of the tradition of reversing roles are to be found in the play with a woman, Viola, dressing up as a man and a servant, Malvolio, imagining that he has become a nobleman.

Although Tchaikovsky's ballet, *The Nutcracker*, is always associated with Christmas, it was first performed in the spring of 1892.

Christmas films and television programmes

Santa's first appearance in a film dates back to 1899 since when he has appeared numerous times. Most Christmas films with a Father Christmas figure are decidedly schmaltzy and amongst the most memorable of these must be *Miracle on 34th Street*, the original version of which appeared in 1947.

And on the subject of schmaltzy Christmas films, many people today wonder just why it is that the film *It's a Wonderful Life* is considered such an icon. In fact this film was something of a flop when it was released in 1946. However, because it had flopped at the box office, its copyright was allowed to lapse thus enabling television companies around the world to rerun it *ad nauseum* without having to pay anything for the privilege, hence its constant appearance in the Christmas television schedules!

But the best script of all for a Christmas film was probably the one written by Charles Dickens. Not that he realised he was writing a film script, he thought he was writing a book – *The Christmas Carol*. It was published in 1843 and was an immediate bestseller, selling 6,000 copies on Christmas Day of that year alone. In the following year nine theatres in London staged dramatised versions of the story and, since then, there have been at least 25 different film versions of it, the first one dating back to 1901. People who have played the part of Ebenezer Scrooge include Alastair Sim (1951), Basil Rathbone (1954), Albert Finney (1970), Mickey Mouse (1983), George C Scott (1984), Bill Murray (1988) and Michael Caine (1992). Strangely, in this most heartwarming of Christmas stories, there is no Father Christmas character.

Telling stories around the hearth is another very ancient midwinter custom. It was also the time when ghost stories were traditionally told. Forget any ideas you may have about telling ghost stories at Halloween – in times past that would have been considered too dangerous a time for such stories as this was when the ghosts roamed the world. Instead Christmas, with its religious associations, used to be considered a particularly safe time to tell ghost stories. This was why, when he wrote a special story for Christmas, Charles Dickens made it a ghost story.

Before Charles Dickens chose the name of Tiny Tim in *A Christmas Carol*, he first thought of using Little Larry, Puny Pete and Small Sam.

Santa, however, hasn't always been a benevolent figure in films. Numerous film baddies have disguised themselves as Santa before committing heinous crimes. But it's not just the baddies who disguise themselves – I've always enjoyed the scene in *The French Connection* where the New York detective played by Gene Hackman disguises himself as Santa during a stakeout.

A rather over-the-top Christmas film featuring Santa was a Sci-Fi film called *Santa Claus Conquers the Martians* which came out in 1964. One reviewer, on seeing it, commented that this film proved that *it's possible to insult the intelligence of a three-year-old.*

These days most of us watch our Christmas films on television rather than at the cinema and there are many perennial Christmas favourites such as *The Sound of Music* and *The Great Escape* that have nothing whatsoever to do with Christmas. Quite often television programmes that appear regularly all through the year have Christmas specials and these tend to gather enormous audiences. A special Christmas episode of *Only Fools and Horses* in 1989 was seen by an audience of over 20 million people. Mind you, the numbers for that programme had been beaten three years earlier when nearly 28 million watched a Christmas episode of *East Enders* in which Dirty Den told Angie he wanted a divorce – very seasonal, I must say!

But for many of us it is the special Christmas variety programmes that we enjoy most and reigning supreme amongst those must be the *Morecambe and Wise Show*; the 1977 show was watched by over 21 million people and, I should think, by countless more in the years since then, as at least one of these shows seems to be repeated every year!

In a poll in 2010 *Home Alone* was voted the greatest family Christmas film of all time. Despite being a flop when it first came out *It's a Wonderful Life* was second, having been first in many previous polls.

A recent poll to discover the worst ever Christmas movie was won by *Jingle All the Way* which starred Arnold Schwarzenegger and came out in 1996.

The first BBC children's charity appeal was a five-minute radio broadcast aired in 1927. It raised £1,143.

The Queen's Christmas broadcast

It was King George V who made the first royal Christmas broadcast (on radio) in 1932. He had first been asked to make a Christmas broadcast in 1923 but had refused. Then, when the BBC got a Royal Charter in 1932, he was again asked by John (later Lord) Reith, the Director-General of the BBC. This time, the idea was accepted. That first broadcast was made from Sandringham. The time of 3pm was chosen for the broadcast because it was considered to be the best time for world-wide (or, in this case, Empire-wide) coverage. At this time all such broadcasts were made live and George V hated doing the broadcast as he was so nervous – he always said that the anticipation of having to give the speech ruined his Christmas dinner.

There was no Christmas broadcast in 1936. Instead Edward VIII made a radio broadcast on 11 December to announce his abdication. George VI then made his first Christmas broadcast in 1937. He suffered from a severe stammer which he had to overcome each year as his broadcasts, too, were always live.

Queen Elizabeth II still continues the tradition begun by her grandfather. With the introduction of televisions to many households, the broadcasts were televised from 1957 so that, by the end of the 1950s, more than half the population of Britain would sit down to watch the Christmas message. It's difficult to estimate just how many people around the globe watch the Queen's message each year; it must be many many millions when you consider that in the United Kingdom alone she regularly gets an audience of nearly 20 million people.

The programme is no longer transmitted live. The last live broadcast took place in 1959 and nowadays the Queen records her message a few days before Christmas Day – so that, unlike her grandfather George V, she at least can enjoy her Christmas dinner.

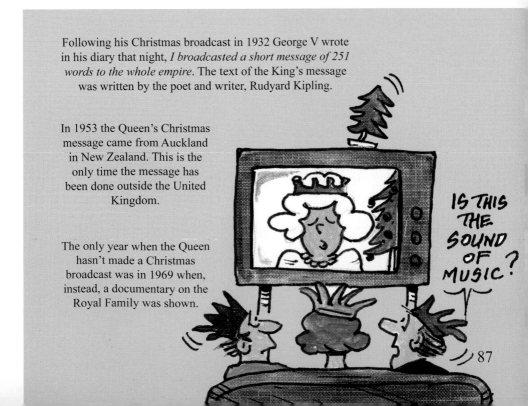

Following his Christmas broadcast in 1932 George V wrote in his diary that night, *I broadcasted a short message of 251 words to the whole empire*. The text of the King's message was written by the poet and writer, Rudyard Kipling.

In 1953 the Queen's Christmas message came from Auckland in New Zealand. This is the only time the message has been done outside the United Kingdom.

The only year when the Queen hasn't made a Christmas broadcast was in 1969 when, instead, a documentary on the Royal Family was shown.

IS THIS THE SOUND OF MUSIC?

10
The build-up to Christmas

Christmas is coming, and the geese are getting fat.
Who'll put a penny in the poor man's hat?
If you have no penny, then a farthing will do.
If you have no farthing, then God bless you.

25 March – Lady Day

A baby's life begins with its conception and so, when we talk about dates that are associated with Christmas, we should really begin with Lady Day.

As it's in the spring that new life, in both plants and animals, begins to appear, traditionally it was in spring at the time of the Equinox that our calendar year began. It was Julius Caesar who first changed things when he introduced his new calendar that began with the month of January. However, many societies within and beyond the Roman Empire continued to use the Spring Equinox as the marker for when each year began, including members of that new religion called Christianity.

It wasn't until the 4th century that the Pope brought the Christian calendar into line with the Roman one. And it was then, too, that the decision was made to celebrate Christ's birth on 25 December by counting nine months from the former beginning of the year.

Today we still celebrate the conception of the Infant Jesus on *Lady Day* or the day of *The Annunciation of Mary*.

Stir Up Sunday

Stir up, we beseech thee,
The pudding in the pot,
And when we get home,
We'll eat the lot.

So says one rhyme but, in fact, the Sunday nearest to St Andrew's Day is really known as Stir Up Sunday because the Collect for the day reads, *Stir up, we beseech Thee, O Lord, the wills of thy faithful people; that they, plenteously bringing forth the fruit of good words, may of these be plenteously rewarded; through Jesus Christ our Lord.*

But the term has also become linked with baking so that this is therefore the day on which you should make your Christmas pudding.

Advent

Advent Sunday is always the nearest Sunday to the
Feast of St Andrew, whether before or after.
(The Book of Common Prayer)

The word *advent* comes from the Latin word *adventus* meaning *the coming* and it refers to the coming of the birth of Jesus on 25 December. It starts on the Sunday closest to 30 November, St Andrew's Day. This means that the length of Advent can vary each year and can sometimes start in November and sometimes not until a few days into December.

There are a number of traditions, most of which have now died out, that were associated with this period. In some places, for example, it was a time for fasting (in view of the feasting to come, this was probably an excellent idea!) and the celebration of marriages was prohibited during Advent.

In Normandy, in France, there was once a tradition that farmers would send out their children with flaming torches to drive away all evil. They would set fire to bundles of hay and straw in order to banish mice and other destructive animals. But only children under the age of twelve were thought to be innocent enough to take part, and I can't help wondering how many unintended fires were also started on these forays.

In the 5th century Advent began on 11 November, St Martin's Day. You then had a six-week fast until Christmas. In Poland the fast would begin after you had feasted on this day by eating goose.

Gerhard Lang's company producing Advent calendars reached a peak of production in the late 1920s and early 1930s by which time he was producing many different calendar designs. It was also Lang who introduced the first Advent calendars with chocolates in them.

It's an old German tradition that children should write letters to the Christ Child on the first Sunday of Advent, and perhaps this is where we get our tradition today whereby children write their letters to Santa.

Advent Calendars are another German tradition and the earliest known version of an Advent calendar dates from 1851. The first specially printed Advent calendars were produced by Gerhard Lang. When he was a child his mother had made him a little calendar for Advent with 24 candles pictured on it. Lang later produced a number of little coloured pictures that people could buy to stick on their own calendars. His first printed calendars (without the little windows that we open today) were marketed in 1908.

The Second World War forced Lang to close his business, and it wasn't until 1946 that Advent calendars were produced once more. By then the idea had crossed the Atlantic to America, and today children all the world over count down the days to Christmas with the help of such calendars. However, these calendars all begin on the first day of December, regardless of when Advent actually starts, and now it is possible to purchase calendars that seem to ignore Christmas altogether and continue the countdown until New Year's Eve instead.

4 December – St Barbe's Day

In Provence, in the south of France, this date marks the beginning of the Christmas festivities and children then sow wheat seeds on tissue paper. If the seeds have germinated by Christmas Day it's a promise of prosperity and a good harvest in the coming year.

6 December – St Nicholas's Day

It is St Nicholas, of course, who lives on in our traditions today as Santa Claus, but, perhaps surprisingly, his saint's day isn't Christmas Day but 6 December.

St Nicholas was Bishop of Myra in Turkey in the 4th century. One day, so one story goes, he heard that the governor of the city had taken a bribe to condemn three innocent men to death. Their executions were just about to take place, when Nicholas arrived on the scene and forced the governor to admit that the men were innocent, and they were therefore spared.

A shrine was built in his memory in Myra and was a centre of pilgrimage until, in 1087, some Italian sailors stole his remains and took them to Bari where a new shrine was built in St Stephen's church. It's said that on the first day after his remains were deposited here, 30 people visiting the shrine were cured of various ills.

Another story about St Nicholas relates how the landlord of an inn in Myra killed three boys and used them as meat in his pies. Fortunately, Nicholas realised what had happened and, by making the sign of the cross over the pies, he brought the boys back to life. It was for this reason that he became the patron saint of children, so that today in many parts of the world it's on St Nicholas's Day that children receive their Christmas presents.

Perhaps the men whose lives he saved in Myra were sailors for St Nicholas is also the patron saint of sailors. He's the patron saint of the countries of Russia and Greece and the cities of Aberdeen and Amsterdam. He's the patron, too, of travellers, dockers, coopers,

The three gold balls that are the traditional sign of pawnbrokers are said to represent three bags of gold that St Nicholas once gave to save three girls from slavery.

In medieval times there was a tradition of electing Boy Bishops in the cathedrals on 6 December each year. The boy would be ordained and wear the vestments of a full bishop and carry out all the duties of a bishop except for taking mass. He acted as bishop in this way until 28 December (Holy Innocents Day). Abolished by Henry VIII in 1541, the custom was briefly brought back again only to be abolished once more in the reign of Queen Elizabeth I, so that by the end of the 16th century it had died out virtually everywhere.

Incidentally, if the Boy Bishop died while he was acting as Bishop, he would be buried with all the honours of a proper bishop. There are one or two effigies of just such boy bishops that survive in churches around the country.

brewers, pilgrims and safe journeys and of perfumiers and pawnbrokers – a very suitable association for Christmas. He is also, incidentally, the patron saint of judges, murderers and thieves – a delightful if confusingly contradictory association, to my mind!

12 December – Feast of Our Lady of Guadaloupe

One of Mexico's most important religious festivals, this commemorates the appearance, in 1531, of the Virgin Mary to a young boy.

13 December – St Lucia's Day

In Sweden the Christmas season begins on this date. The oldest daughter in the household gets up early and dresses in white. Wearing a wreath with seven lighted candles on her head she then serves other members of the family coffee and buns in bed. For many years St Lucia's Day was only celebrated in isolated parts of Sweden. Then, in the 1920s, a Stockholm newspaper arranged a competition to choose a Lucia bride to represent the city. The idea caught hold and nowadays every school, office or club in the country chooses a Lucia bride at this time of year.

St Lucia (or St Lucy) is the patron saint of light and blindness, hence the candles that are always associated with her day.

21 December – St Thomas's Day, the winter solstice

The day of St Thomas, the blessed divine,
Is good for brewing, baking and killing fat swine.

This is, of course, the shortest day and longest night of the year. In some parts of the country it was also the day when money would be paid from charity boxes to the poor so that collecting money or food for charity on this day was sometimes known as *Thomasing*.

In the village of Bolingbroke in Lincolnshire a candle auction was held on this date each year. The vicar would stick a pin into a lit candle and then accept bids from local farmers for the grazing rights on land in the parish, the money going to charity. Eventually the candle would melt and the pin fall down – the last bid received before this happened would be the winning bid and that farmer would then be the tenant of the land for the coming year.

These days many schools have already closed for the Christmas holidays by the time 21 December comes around. However, there used to be a custom whereby on this date, for perhaps the only day in the year, schoolchildren would actually race to be first to get to school – because if they got there before the schoolmaster, on this day at least, they would then be able to bar the teacher from the school and have the day off.

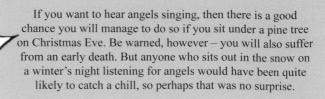

If you want to hear angels singing, then there is a good chance you will manage to do so if you sit under a pine tree on Christmas Eve. Be warned, however – you will also suffer from an early death. But anyone who sits out in the snow on a winter's night listening for angels would have been quite likely to catch a chill, so perhaps that was no surprise.

24 December – Christmas Eve

Christmas Eve is, of course, when Father Christmas travels all over the globe in his sleigh pulled by his team of reindeer. There are a number of traditions associated specifically with animals on this date. A well-known one is that all the animals can speak in human tongues when midnight strikes – but it's extremely unlucky to attempt to listen to them. A tradition from Jersey, in the Channel Islands, says that it's unlucky to enter a cowshed at midnight on Christmas Eve, probably for this very reason

Another tradition states that all the animals kneel at midnight, and yet another says that cattle all turn and face to the east (towards Bethlehem). In Herefordshire it's said that it's only seven-year old cattle that do this, because that was the age of the oxen in the stable where Jesus was born.

All the cocks are supposed to crow throughout Christmas Eve to proclaim His birth. Woe betide any poor dog that starts howling because of the noise – it risks being shot because dogs that howl on Christmas Eve will certainly go mad before the New Year begins. Even bees are involved – they are said to wake up from their winter hibernation to hum the Hundredth Psalm in their hives before going back to sleep.

But not all traditions on Christmas Eve are associated with animals. Bread baked on that day was once thought to be good for those suffering from diarrhoea and dysentery, so sometimes extra bread would be baked on Christmas Eve. This would then be dried and crushed into powder and kept for use as a medicine in the future. It was said to be especially potent if it had been moistened with Christmas dew.

Christmas Eve was traditionally a day of fasting in many Roman Catholic countries – hence the tradition also of attending Midnight Mass and then feasting straight afterwards. In France this feast was known as *La Réveillon* while in Germany at such a feast an extra place would be laid at the table for the Virgin Mary because there was no room for her at the inn.

Finally, Christmas Eve was the date on which you brought your **Yule Log** into the house and lit it. *Yule* was the old Norse word for the Viking mid-winter festival which, like so many others, became interlinked with the Christian Christmas when the pagan Vikings were converted.

The Yule log was traditionally a large, single log of wood, big enough to burn for the twelve days of Christmas – remember, this tradition dates from a time when there would have been a single enormous fireplace in the heart of the house. Before Christmas, the members of the household would have gone out into the countryside to search for a suitable log to drag home – incidentally, a Yule log should never be bought; it should be found on your own land or else given to you.

At the end of the festivities, a small piece of the old Yule log should be saved from the fire and kept to protect the household from fire and lightning in the coming year.

Tolling the church bells for Midnight Mass announces the death of the Devil and the coming of Christ.

Irish legend has it that at midnight the gates of Paradise open so that anyone who dies at that time goes straight to Heaven. Elsewhere it is said that ghosts and witches have no power to harm anyone on Christmas Eve.

There's a link between yule logs and slavery in America. Apparently, some slaves' contracts (did they have such things?) specified that they should have seven days' rest over Christmas, or as long as it took the yule log to burn. Consequently, before the celebrations began the slaves would soak the log in water in order to make it last as long as possible. A saying then evolved that described a water-logged piece of wood as having as much water as a Christmas log.

11
The twelve days of Christmas

It was agreed in our part of the firing line that there would be no firing and no thought of war on Christmas Eve and Christmas Day ... on Christmas Day a football match was played between them and us in front of the trench. They even allowed us to bury all our dead.
(A member of the London Rifle Brigade writing about the 1914 ceasefire on the western front)

25 December – Christmas Day

People who are born on Christmas Day are said to be particularly favoured and gifted. This was certainly true of Isaac Newton who was born on Christmas Day in 1642.

The Pope delivers his annual Christmas blessing, known as the *Urbi et Orbi*, in the Vatican at noon on Christmas Day. The term, literally, means *to the City (of Rome) and to the World*, and was a standard opening for proclamations in the time of the Roman Empire.
This, and another such blessing at Easter, is broadcast to the world and by it, remission and forgiveness of sins is granted by the Pope not only to those people present in St Peter's Square but also to those watching the ceremony on television or listening on the radio.

Christmas Day anniversaries

AD 800   Charlemagne crowned by Pope Leo III as Emperor of the Romans, thus establishing the Holy Roman Empire which was to last for 1,000 years.

1066   William the Conqueror crowned in Westminster Abbey after his victory at the Battle of Hastings.

1085   William the Conqueror ordered a survey of land ownership – later known as the *Domesday Book.*

1176   The first Welsh Eisteddfod took place at Cardigan Castle.

1620   Landing at Plymouth Rock, Massachusetts, of the Pilgrim Fathers.

1771   Dorothy Wordsworth, the writer and sister of the more famous William, was born.

1868   Linus Yale, the inventor of the Yale Lock died.

1899   Humphrey Bogart, the actor and star of such films as *Casablanca* and *The African Queen,* was born.

1906   Lew Grade, the theatrical impresario who brought *The Muppets* to our television screens, was born.

1914   A football match took place between Germany and the Allies during an unauthorised ceasefire in World War One.

1932   George V made the first Royal Christmas broadcast.

1932   Little Richard, the rock singer, best known for songs like *Tutti Fruiti* and *Long Tall Sally,* was born.

1936   Princess Alexandra was born.

1941   Hong Kong surrendered to the Japanese.

1946   WC Fields, the actor, best known for his catchphrase, *There's a sucker born every minute,* died.

1972   President Harry S Truman died.

1977   Charlie Chaplin, star of many films including *The Gold Rush* and *The Great Dictator,* died.

1990   A successful trial run was carried out on the system that would become the World Wide Web.

Along some parts of the Western Front the unofficial truce in 1914 lasted for up to six weeks, with Allied and German troops exchanging cigarettes and food. The military authorities (on both sides) didn't know how to respond to this outbreak of peace amongst their soldiers, so the following year strict orders were given before Christmas that there was to be no fraternisation with the enemy. The truce was never repeated.

The word Noel or *Nowell* comes from the Latin *natalis* meaning birth. Consequently, the state of Natal in South Africa is so-called because it was discovered by Vasco da Gama on Christmas Day in 1497. Similarly, Christmas Island in the Indian Ocean was discovered on Christmas Day in 1642 and it was on Christmas Day 1777 that Captain Cook landed on the other Christmas Island in the Pacific Ocean; it is also known as Kiritimati.

A rather sad fact associated with Christmas is that haemophilia is sometimes known as the *Christmas Disease*, because Christmas was the surname of one of the first people treated for it after it had been diagnosed.

26 December – St Stephen's Day or Boxing Day

Good King Wenceslas looked out
On the feast of Stephen

St Stephen, to whom this day is dedicated, was a Jew living in Jerusalem at the time of Jesus' crucifixion. When, in AD 35, he spoke of Jesus (after His death and resurrection) standing on the right hand of God, he was condemned for blasphemy and stoned to death making him one of Christianity's first martyrs. His death was watched (and approved of) by a man called Saul. Saul was later to become a Christian convert himself and to be much better known to history as St Paul.

As for the day's other name of Boxing Day – after working for their masters all day on Christmas Day itself, the servants would get their reward on this day with a holiday of their own. Not only did they get the day off but the poor of the parish would be given money – this was traditionally the day that the almsboxes in the churches were opened and the money shared amongst the poor – and this is one of the reasons why we now know it as Boxing Day.

There is another reason – it wasn't just church almsboxes that were opened. Traditionally on this day servants and tradesmen would go around households they worked for asking for tips in boxes they carried for the purpose. As early as the 1830s this practice was being criticised in the press since many people abused the system, and this possibly gave rise to the growing practice of people giving money to charity at this time instead.

You will, however, find references to the fact that it is so called because boxing matches were held on this day; certainly it was a day for sporting activities (especially hunting) but this is not the reason for the name. Incidentally, this date in Australia always sees the start of the Sydney to Hobart yacht race.

Is Boxing Day the first day after Christmas Day or is it, if Christmas should fall on a Saturday, not until the following Monday? It would appear that not even the experts agree as *The Oxford Dictionary* says it refers to the first weekday after Christmas whereas *The Oxford Book of Days* says that it is always the day after Christmas regardless of when Christmas itself falls.

King Henry VIII passed a law banning the playing of sport on Christmas Day. This law has never officially been repealed. Perhaps this explains why so many sporting fixtures have traditionally taken place on Boxing Day.

Christmas boxes were once made in the form of hollow clay balls with a slit at the top for the coins. This meant that they had to be smashed to be opened so that no-one could open them before the due date.

The first official Boxing Day Bank Holiday was in 1871.

The term *Boxing Day* may be a comparatively recent invention, dating back only to the 1830s. One of the earliest recorded uses of the term is found in Dickens's *The Pickwick Papers* when Sam Weller proclaims, *No man ever talked poetry 'cept a beadle on boxin' day*.

In the Bahamas 26 December is known as *Junkanoo* and celebrates freedom from slavery. It is named after a slave master called John Canoe.

28 December – Holy Innocents Day

Then Herod, when he saw that he was mocked of the wise men,
was exceeding wroth, and sent forth, and slew all the children
that were in Bethlehem, and in all the coasts thereof,
from two years old and under, according to the time
which he had diligently enquired of the wise men.
(Matthew, Chapter 2)

Never ever start a new project on 28 December – traditionally, it is said to be the unluckiest day of the year. Holy Innocents Day, as it is called, commemorates the infants that were put to death on the orders of King Herod.

The King had been visited by the three wise men, who had told him they were looking for a new-born King of the Jews as foretold by a bright star. Wanting to ensure that there was no future competition from such a King, Herod ordered that every male child under the age of two should be killed. Warned of King Herod's plans in a dream, Joseph escaped with his wife and the child to safety in Egypt.

King Herod's insistence on the slaying of all the baby boys has always seemed an incredible action but recent archaeological research has shown that such slaughter actually did take place. An excavation at Ashkelon, not far from Bethlehem, has revealed a mass grave with around 100 infants in it. Some of the babies were newborn, some a little older, most were male (it's not always possible to discover the sex of such small children from purely osteological evidence) and, sure enough, the burial dates from the period when Herod was king.

Certainly King Herod was known for his cruelty and would have been quite capable of ordering the deaths of all the baby boys in the region. Moreover, one record of the time described Herod as someone *who kills the princes by the sword, who kills them in secret places so that no one knows where to find the bodies, who kills the old and young ones, without mercy*. This last comment might even have been a reference to the massacre of the baby boys.

King Herod even had his own son murdered so that Augustus Caesar is alleged to have said, *Better to be Herod's pig than Herod's son.*

King Herod's Day Observation Society
All Children under Two will be thrown Overboard
(Sign on board a troopship carrying soldiers and their families in the 1950s!)

Should auld acquaintance be forgot,
And never brought to min'?
Should auld acquaintance be forgot
And days of auld lang syne?
And for auld lang syne, my dear,
For auld land syne,
We'll tak a cup o' kindness yet,
For auld lang syne.
(Robert Burns)

The word *hogmanay* means the *last day of the year*. It comes from a Norman French word *hoguinané*.

31 December – New Year's Eve

Old lang syne (meaning *old long ago*) is a poem of love and friendship in times past. The well-known ballad was written by Robert Burns shortly before his death in 1796 at the age of 37, and it's thought by some that Burns had a premonition of his death when he wrote it; he was certainly already suffering from ill-health.

Today, the song is always sung just after the clock has signalled the start of a new year or at the end of gatherings with people holding hands in a circle. When this particular part of the tradition originated isn't known, but it may come from words in the last verse, *And there's a hand my trusty fiere! And gie's a hand o' thine!* The music is thought to be an old Scottish dance tune, and holding hands may also have been part of the dance that went with it.

1 January – New Year's Day

The month of January is named for the god, Janus, god of beginnings, doors and gates. Janus had two faces, in order to look forward and back, since a door can let you in or let you out. The first month of the year is named after him because this is a time when people look back on the year just ended, and forward to the year to come.

5 January – Twelfth Night

Christmas Day was the morning of the season:
New Year's Day the middle of it or noon;
Twelfth Night is the night.
(Leigh Hunt 1840)

There are twelve days of Christmas. The first is Christmas Day and if you then count to twelve, the Twelfth Night must be 5 January. The next day is Epiphany. Nowadays, however, the two events seem to have become one in most people's minds.

6 January – Epiphany

When they saw the star, they rejoiced with exceeding great joy.
(Matthew, Chapter 2)

The word *Epiphany* means *manifestation*. In other words, this day recalls the day on which the Baby Jesus was manifested or shown to the world, in this case to the three wise men.

For some Christians, Epiphany is more important than Christmas Day, because it reminds us that Jesus, born a Jew, was sent to the world by God for all of us. The wise men were not Jews and they therefore represent all people of the world – this also explains why, in many paintings for example, the three wise men are invariably shown as representing different races.

But Twelfth Night was also the last night of the Christmas celebrations. This was your last chance to party before life returned to normal. As a result, parties on this night tended to be riotous affairs.

These parties were presided over by a King and Queen of Misrule, a tradition that apparently goes back to the 14th century. They would be chosen when everyone ate a slice of Twelfth Night cake within which was hidden a bean and a pea. Whoever found the bean would be King, and whoever found the pea would be Queen.

Other things were hidden in the cake as well – if you found a clove you were a villain, a twig and you were a fool, and no girl wanted to find a bit of rag in her slice of cake because that implied she was no better than she should be!

The impersonation of a king and a queen, chosen from beans and peas in cakes, is an essential element of the topsy-turvy tradition of Twelfth Night, when the lowest were raised to the top and were served by their betters, even if only for a short time. We saw this idea also behind the boy bishops and the tradition of schoolboys throwing out their master on the 21 December. In some regiments the same topsy-turvy world was acknowledged on Christmas Day when officers would ceremoniously serve their men at dinner.

7 January

In Ethiopia it is on this date that the Coptic Church celebrates Christmas. The same is true for the Russian Orthodox church. However, the Russian church reckons its days from sunset to sunset – as their Christmas Day is on 7 January their celebrations for Christmas therefore begin with sunset on 6 January.

In some parts of North America people have Twelfth Night fires when they burn their Christmas trees.

There was a tradition in the West Country that, at some time during the first week of January, people should go wassailing in their orchards – to keep away bad spirits and encourage the trees to bear fruit later in the year.

12
Christmas traditions from around the world

Wherever Englishmen are on 25ᵗʰ December, there is Christmas. Whether it be in the icy regions of Arctic zones, or in the sweltering heat of tropical sunshine…
(WF Dawson, 1902)

As we have seen, there are hundreds of traditions associated with Christmas from all over the world, many of them travelling around the globe as people have moved from one place to another and taken their customs with them.

There are also many traditions that remain linked to a specific part of the world. One such tradition within the United Kingdom is to be found in **Scotland** with the *first-footers*. A first-footer is the first person to step through the door of a household after midnight, as the New Year begins, bringing good luck to the household. To bring his good luck the person who first-foots should always be male. However, he shouldn't be cross-eyed, flat-footed, blind or lame. Different parts of Scotland have different ideas about what hair colouring is lucky. It is possible, however, to cancel any bad luck from a first-footer by sprinkling salt on your fire.

A number of other rules apply – the first-footer should enter the house by the front door and bring with him coal, bread and salt. These symbolise warmth, life and hospitality. Sometimes first-footers are also expected to carry a sprig of evergreen and some mistletoe. Having come through the front door the first-footer should then leave by the back door, thus taking his good luck right through the house.

> In Sweden Christmas always begins with a church service on St Lucia's Day, the 13th December. The service starts with a procession of adults and children carrying candles into the church and led by a girl wearing a crown of candles.

The tradition that the first-footer arriving in Scottish homes should be dark probably dates back to the time when a fair-haired visitor could have been a Viking warrior coming to attack you.

Sometimes, instead of bread and salt, a first-footer brings whisky and a bannock – again to ensure that members of the household don't starve in the coming year.

In **Scandinavia** Christmas starts with *Christingle* (which means *Christ Light*) on 13 December. Candles are lit at this time to represent Jesus as the light of the world. Actually the first documented Christingle service took place in Germany on Christmas Eve of 1747. At the service each child was given a lit candle tied with red ribbon to remind him or her of Jesus and the blood He shed to save mankind. Today's Christingle candles are usually placed in an orange (to represent the world) and are decorated with fruits and sweets attached with four cocktail sticks and these represent God's gifts through the four seasons of the year.

Also in Sweden, Christmas Eve was often known as *Dipping Day* because many families would go through the ritual of *doppa y grytan*. In other words they would dip rye bread in the hot cooking liquid produced from the Christmas ham – which sounds really delicious.

The burning of Advent Candles is a tradition that comes from **Denmark**. The candle was marked with 24 lines, to signify each of the days until Christmas and would be lit each day to burn from one line down to the next. In **Ireland**, on the other hand, a candle is often placed in a window on Christmas Eve to guide the Holy Family to shelter.

In **Poland**, Christmas Eve is called *The Festival of the Star* and on that evening children watch out for the first star to appear in the sky, a reminder of the star of Bethlehem. Another reminder of the first Christmas that is followed in many parts of eastern Europe is to place a sheaf of corn on the table – this reminds everyone that Jesus was born in a stable.

In the **United States** many Americans combine Christmas with *Kwanzaa*, an Afro-American holiday which lasts for seven days from 26 December. On each day, families light a candle symbolising one of seven principles, including creativity, faith and unity. The name Kwanzaa means *first fruits* and the celebration is closely associated with the harvest.

When *Sinter Klaas* (Santa) visited households in **Holland** on 6 December rather than on Christmas Eve he was always accompanied by a servant called *Swarte Piet* (Black Peter). As in Britain, presents were left for all the good children but, in Holland, Swarte Piet would leave a birch rod for those children who had been naughty during the year. In **Germany** there is a similar tradition, but here the person who leaves the rod is called *Knecht Ruprecht* (Servant Rupert). In **Scandinavian countries** it is often an elf who delivers the presents for Santa – his name is *Julenissen* (in Norway and Denmark) or *Jultomten* (in Sweden). The first element of this name is, once again, linked with the word *Yule*, the old name given to Scandinavia's mid-winter festivities.

I'm sure there are many parents, faced with the expense of buying endless toys on behalf of Santa, who would be glad to see the tradition come to an end. But would they go so far as those clergymen in **France** who, in the 1950s, burnt an effigy of *Père Noel* (Father Christmas) because they felt he was a satanic figure?

In **Greece** gift-giving is reserved for New Year's Day (St Basil's Day) and it is St Basil who comes down the chimney with the present. Strangely enough, although St Nicholas is Greece's patron saint, he's not associated in this country with giving presents.

On the evening of 5 January children in **Spain** leave their shoes on a balcony or near a window so that the wise men can leave presents for them on their way to visit the infant Jesus. The same thing happens in **Italy,** only here the presents are left by a kindly old witch called *la Befana*. The story is that la Befana was invited to travel to Bethlehem with the wise men but refused, saying that she was too busy cleaning her house, and so she missed out on the opportunity to see the Christ Child.

Unlike la Befana, *Babushka* in **Russia** was a wicked old witch who, when la Befana changed her mind and wanted to catch up with the wise men, gave her the wrong directions. Babushka was therefore condemned to roam all over Russia on the eve of Epiphany giving presents to all good children. Sadly for Russia's children, she was outlawed by the Communists because of her religious associations but she is now making a comeback.

Another tradition about Babushka relates how she, too, was visited by the wise men and, like la Befana, decided she was too busy cleaning her house to go with them. Later she changed her mind, but by this time the snow had covered their footprints and so she didn't know which way to go. By the time she found her way to Bethlehem the Holy Family had already gone to Egypt and so she laid some black bread that she had baked in the manger and returned home. Consequently, children in Russia may find a piece of black bread (wrapped in coloured paper) at the bottom of their stockings.

In parts of **Latin America** it is also the tradition for children to receive their presents on the eve of Epiphany. In **Mexico** the children will play a game for their presents – a paper or clay figure called a *piñata* is filled with sweets and small presents and hung up. The children are then blindfolded and take it in turns to try and hit the piñata with a stick until eventually it breaks, and out fall all the goodies.

La Befana (who brings gifts to children in Italy) gets her name from an early corruption of the word *Epiphany*.

Of course, in many of these countries Christmas falls in wintertime, when hot roast turkey and warming punches are very welcome as you sit down to feast. In the southern hemisphere, however, on a hot, sunny day when you want to go to the beach, it's not exactly the kind of meal that is going to appeal to everyone. Consequently, in **Australia** in recent years it has become the custom for many people to celebrate Christmas in December with a barbecue and then have a second *Christmas in July* with a hot roast-turkey-with-all-the-trimmings meal when it is cooler.

It doesn't matter where you go in the world, each region has special stories and traditions that are associated with our modern celebration of Christmas. Not all of them are the same and I'm sure many of your own traditions will differ from those that I have described above. Trying to unravel all of them and discover how they originated has been a joyous task and I hope, you too, will find that you enjoy each Christmas more as you understand it better.

Finally, may I wish you all *A Merry Christmas!*

God bless us every one!
(Tiny Tim, in Charles Dickens's *A Christmas Carol*)